D1424226

POSITIVE
PAPERBACKS

Babies!
A Parents' Guide to Surviving (and Enjoying!) Baby's First Year
Christopher Green

The First Five Minutes
You May Never Get a Second Chance to Make a First Impression
Norman King

The Food Pharmacy
Dramatic New Evidence that Food is Your Best Medicine
Jean Carper

The Good Marriage
A Guide to Getting Wed and Enjoying Marriage in Modern Times
Helen Garlick and Jane Stuart Sheppard

Intangible Evidence
Exploring the Paranormal World and Developing Your Psychic Skills
Bernard Gittelson

Loveshock
How to Recover From a Broken Heart and Love Again
Stephen Gullo Ph.D and Connie Church

Necessary Losses
The Loves, Illusions, Dependencies and Impossible Expectations That All
of Us Have to Give Up in Order to Grow
Judith Viorst

The Power of Your Subconscious Mind
Dr Joseph Murphy

60 Second Shiatzu
How to Energise, Erase Pain and Conquer Tension in One Minute
Eva Shaw

Talk Language
How to Use Conversation for Profit and Pleasure
Allan Pease with Alan Garner

The Tao of Health, Sex and Longevity
A Modern, Practical Approach to the Ancient Way
Daniel Reid

Unlimited Power
Anthony Robbins

Who Needs God
Harold Kushner

The Working Mother's Survival Guide
Jill Black

SELF-HELP FROM SIMON & SCHUSTER

* * *

60-Second Shiatzu

* * *

How to Energize, Erase Pain, and Conquer Tension in One Minute

Eva Shaw

S I M O N & S C H U S T E R

LONDON·SYDNEY·NEW YORK·TOKYO·SINGAPORE·TORONTO

First published in Great Britain by
Simon & Schuster Ltd in 1990

Reprinted 1990, 1993

First published in the USA by Mills & Sanderson, Publishers,
as a trade paperback.

Chapter illustrations by Jannell Cannon.

Simon & Schuster Ltd
West Garden Place
Kendal Street
London W2 2AQ

Simon & Schuster of Australia Pty Ltd
Sydney

British Library Cataloguing-in-Publication Data available
ISBN 0-671-71504-6

Printed and bound in great Britain by
The Bath Press, Avon

* * *

To Joe and Matt . . .
your support, laughter and love
have made this book a reality.

* * *

ACKNOWLEDGEMENTS

I want to extend my special thanks to:
Sharon Morgan, my mentor, for her ''yes, you can''
attitude;
Joe Shaw, my friend, my husband, my lover, for always
believing;
and to Georgia Mills, my publisher, for helping me
polish
60-Second Shiatzu.

CONTENTS

60-Second Shiatzu

Introduction

You're an active, intelligent adult. Go ahead, admit it—you're dedicated to an exciting career. At the same time, you're also sampling all the pleasure and stimulation life has to offer. Why not—you work hard and you play hard—you deserve the best.

When things are going well, you feel like the world's on *your* string. But there are side effects to this good life—fatigue, tension, even that "wrung out" feeling. They creep in unnoticed, and before you realize what's happening you have a migraine, an upset stomach, a stiff neck, or a tight jaw.

Would you like to do more than temporarily relieve the aches of the eighties? Wouldn't you rather know how to eradicate them from your life? Do you want to energize, ease pain, and conquer tension in one minute? Shiatzu is your answer.

Shiatzu is easy and you can learn it right now.

Is your head a bit achy? Just hold your left hand out in front of you. Now place your right thumb on top and your right index finger underneath your left palm in the "web" between the thumb and base of the first finger. As you continue to read the next few paragraphs, simply massage with gentle, circular motions at this shiatzu point using a light amount of pressure.

Relief is on the way. You're sampling shiatzu at this very moment. See—there are no mystical movements to master or complicated techniques to learn. Most of the movements? do them in your street clothes, anytime and anywhere. With a little practice, no one will even know you're recharging the natural, drug-free way.

The movement you're doing now is effective against headaches and toothaches. It's perfect when you want to give it all you've got in a high-intensity sales meeting, when you need a quick pick-me-up at 4:15, or when you're squirming in the dentist chair.

Now switch hands and repeat the same gentle massage on the right hand. Some people find the technique of just applying pressure more satisfactory than massage. On the other hand many who use shiatzu as a tonic in the morning and a relaxer in the evening apply a form of pulsating pressure with amazing results. Do not use so much pressure that it causes discomfort, but definitely use a firm touch.

Shiatzu is based on the Japanese art of massaging and applying pressure to the body on energy lines called meridians. Shiatzu improves health by increasing the flow of energy through the body. With the movements included in this book you can perform these exhilarating techniques in the conference room, in a traffic jam, or in other situations when you're in the grip of tension—today.

If you're tired of popping an aspirin and find it nearly impossible to "get out for exercise" when you're in the middle of a business transaction, an interview, that labor dispute, or any nerve tangling situation, *let shiatzu come to your rescue.*

Shiatzu won't cause pain and should give no more discomfort than working on a sore muscle. You know your body better than anyone and understanding the fine line between pain and pleasure so you can use as much or as little pressure as is comfortable. Because you'll be stimulating points on the meridians and massaging muscles, you will feel a pleasantly warm sensation on the skin surface that spreads to the flesh below, along with the comfortably familiar pressure of your own touch. Shiatzu is your key to vitality and general well-being. It will revitalize a sagging body, promote healing, reduce fatigue, and encourage sound, natural sleep. It's the ultimate stress reliever.

It's not a medication so there's no chance that you'll "OD". Shiatzu may, however, become a life-long habit because:

It's a tonic.

It's a dynamic energy source at your finger tips.

It's quick, easy, and safe.

You'll enjoy doing *60-Second Shiatzu.*

CHAPTER

1

As You Begin...

Quickly skim over the following suggestions and keep them in mind as you add shiatzu to your life.

• There's no need to push hard. Simply apply a firm touch, about as much as you'd use to ring a door bell, hit a manual typewriter key or press out a phone number. But there may also be times, as when in the grip of a throbbing headache, that a deeper, firmer pressure will feel right. Experiment with your fingers and let your personal sense of pleasure and pain guide you.

• Do the moves that feel right to you. Many prefer a solid, stable pressure from their thumb or index finger, while others achieve more effective results with a clockwise, circular massage or a pulsating touch.

• While massage on the shiatzu points will be helpful using either hand, going either direction, traditional shiatzu practitioners prefer using the left hand as much as possible and work left to right when convenient.

• According to shiatzu theory, clockwise massage is to energize the body and counter clockwise massage is to relax it.

• In the text you are frequently told to breathe in a special way; as with yoga, it is suggested that you exhale as much air as possible, then inhale deeply, filling the lower lungs first. This breathing technique allows you to get more air into the lungs and relieves tension, thus boosting the effectiveness of the moves.

• Some shiatzu therapists are very precise about the exact location of each massage point, but for self-massage this book is based on the idea that if you massage or press in a half-dollar-sized area, you will touch the point. Different body sizes also complicate the process of finding exact point locations. Let the professionals worry about the more complicated massage techniques and exact points.

• For the movements in this book, you will normally be either sitting or lying down. If you are comfortable doing them while standing, that is all right, too.

• You may want to go through the moves in privacy the first time to find your favorites before you need them. Since not everyone reacts to fatigue, nervousness, or stress in the same way, use the moves geared to your personal needs. *60-Second Shiatzu* is here to help, not structure your life.

• Try the moves in combination, such as one for a headache, another for a stomach upset, and another to energize all over. Since you won't always be in a heated sales meeting or other group situation when you need shiatzu, master the moves which require more obvious action in addition to the ones you can do discreetly.

• Do not continue with any movements which are uncomfortable or feel awkward, and discontinue any that bring on unexplained discomfort.

• Use either the tips of your fingers and thumbs, or the"finger print" side if your nails are long or if that feels more natural.

• To increase the stimulus of shiatzu, try rubbing your hands together briskly, as if to warm them, before doing any of the movements.

• At times, you might find pinching with your four fingers opposed by your thumb will give you the right amount of pressure on a shiatzu point. You might also discover that gently working the skin back and forth with the thumb or fingers promotes a more pleasing sensation than pressure or pinching. There is no need to cause pain—make the movement fluid and soothing.

• Before beginning shiatzu, you may want to close your eyes, breathe in deeply and exhale smoothly for a moment or two. This technique encourages quick relief and allows the energy lines to flow more easily.

• With these movements, you will at times, apply gentle pressure or massage to the actual area you're treating, while at other times, you'll massage your arm, for example, to alleviate a stomach upset, your thumb for a headache, or your back to relieve hiccoughs. You may even experience a tingling sensation in another part of your body while doing the shiatzu movement for that spot—even though you're actually massaging another area on that energy line (meridian).

• Keep *60-Second Shiatzu* close at hand or copy a few of your "favorite" moves on 3x5 cards and place them in the glove compartment of your car (so you can use shiatzu in a traffic jam), on your nightstand, or inside your middle desk drawer at the office. If you're on a weight loss program, you might increase the effectiveness of the diet by tacking a relaxing move inside your refrigerator to remind you that nervous nibbling adds inches, but shiatzu can help you slim down by eliminating some of the stress from your life. Keep details of these moves close at hand and you're more likely to use them regularly—today, tomorrow, and forever—whenever you want to feel better fast!

• Should you experience unusual or unexplained pain, stop immediately and consult a physician. Keep in mind that shiatzu should improve and enhance your general well-being and is not meant to take the place of professional medical advice.

Many practitioners warn of complications when shiatzu is performed on someone with a terminal illness, cancer, diabetes, heart problems, or bleeding during pregnancy. Discuss the use of shiatzu with your doctor if you have any physical or mental concerns.

This book is not intended to make you a card-carrying shiatzu therapist. Use it as an aid to alternative health care. With this self-help program, you'll get quicker results if you follow these guidelines:

1. Do not eat before doing shiatzu,
2. Avoid using any pain-killers, even aspirin, before treatment,
3. Refrain from working out with your regular exercise program for at least 30 minutes prior to doing your shiatzu moves.

There is no right or wrong way to do shiatzu. You know your body better than anyone and can calculate that fine line between pleasure and pain. Depending on the situation and need, you'll probably use various amounts of pressure. When you have a throbbing headache and massage the hollows on each side of your spine, at the back of your skull, you'll press **hard**, yet when you're releasing tension and boosting your brain power, you'll probably want a smooth, circular, and gentle massage. Review the moves and select the ones which work best for you.

Read through the book and consider the variety of self-treatments. Select the ones you need right at this moment. You don't have to memorize anything—the information is clear and concise. Just read the directions and begin. Why wait another minute to give a supercharge to your stamina, alleviate pain, intensify your energy level, and activate your innate vitality? You already know how to do one shiatzu movement—the others are just as easy, so go ahead and choose shiatzu and help yourself to better health.

Would you enjoy knowing the history of this health-promoting alternative? Are you interested in some scientific facts on the medical applications of shiatzu? Are you wondering how to locate and select a shiatzu therapist in your area? For the history of shiatzu, skip right to Chapter 16,"Yesterday, Today, and Tomorrow." Chapter 17,"Shiatzu—A Safe and Sane Alternative," will give you insight into the ways doctors and nurses have blended shiatzu into their work. Chapter 18,"Locating a Shiatzu Therapist," will provide all the information you need to find a professional therapist to enhance your appreciation of shiatzu, will suggest questions to ask when you locate one, and will provide a glossary of shiatzu terms so you can "speak the language."

CHAPTER

2

Head and Neck

Ask ten different men and women where pain first hits them and nine will probably say in the head—from throbbing migraines to a dull, deep discomfort. Those pains in the head can last from just a few minutes to days. Obviously, they pose significant problems for many of us, especially if they occur frequently.

The time has come to throw out the nonprescription drugs—pills, liquids, and foaming seltzer compounds—which are supposed to be miracle cures. Sure, they can bring relief, but not without possible side effects of an upset stomach, intestinal sluggishness, or that sleepiness you have to avoid like the plague if you want to keep up with the competition. Now there's shiatzu—no pills, no drowsy-droopy feeling, and definitely no after effects, except a feeling of total well-being.

Before using any shiatzu, for headache or stiffness in the neck area, close your eyes and take a few

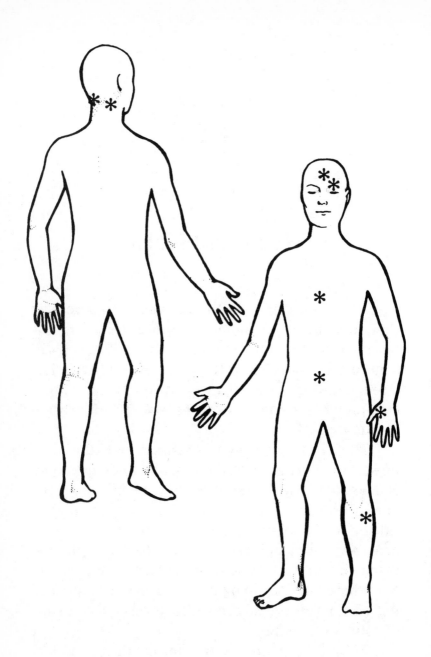

*Location of shiatzu points for Chapter 2 exercises.

deep breaths. While you're relaxing, tune into your body rhythms and silently identify where the tension starts and stops, plus any other discomforts throughout your body, so you can treat them with shiatzu.

It's especially important to realize that you must remove both the symptoms and the cause of your headaches from your life. Yes, headaches or a stiff neck can be brought on by stress, but food sensitivities can play a major role as can undetected toxins in your environment, and even the need for reading glasses. Let shiatzu revitalize you so that you will be able to think clearly and respond with precision, but also use it as a stepping stone to maximum health.

Use the following moves one at a time or in a series of four. With a few minutes of practice, you'll be able to do them without anyone realizing that you're curing a headache and relieving the tension in your neck. There's no need to excuse yourself to take an aspirin and no need to "advertise" that you're not up to par. Unless, that is, you want to share *60-Second Shiatzu*.

• To fight back against a *crushing headache,* and to relax the eyes, follow this routine closely. It can also be used to stop nose bleeds, stabilize blood pressure, and generally improve your sense of well-being.

1. On the back of your neck, find where your spinal column begins. On both sides of this spot are strong muscles, and just slightly further up the sides of the neck are two indentations at the base of the skull.

2. Place your thumbs in the indentations, spreading your fingers in a fan shape on-to your scalp. Press or massage these points with your thumbs for 10 seconds. Relax for a moment and repeat. Within 60 seconds you'll feel a surge of relief.

* * *

• When do you experience a **headache**? After a 12-hour day? When everything has broken loose at the office and the national manager is visiting the next day? When there are problems with the kids? When the budget won't stretch? The pressure inches into your skull, and as your muscles tense you find yourself with a general, ache-all-over headache beating a tom-tom in your head? Master this next movement and put it to work at the on-set of a headache. Keep in mind that it works well even when the pain has a grip on your head, and it allows your head to clear so those creative ideas can flow again.

1. At the base of the skull between the upper-most neck vertebra and the skull is a small hollow. Bend your head forward to locate the vertebra, place a finger there, then bend your head back to discover the hollow.

2. Rub or press a finger or thumb in this area for a slow count of 10. Relax, count to 10 and repeat four more times. Wait five minutes and repeat the entire movement. There's no possibility of overdosing on shiatzu, so make it work for you. Banish pain from your head the shiatzu way.

* * *

• *Headache and eyestrain* unfortunately go together. In the past you've probably tried rubbing your eyes and your forehead to relieve pain (actually a form of pressure massage), but now you can use shiatzu to treat yourself in all the right places. Next time that pain starts and you feel your eyes squinting, try this next movement.

1. Located in the middle portion of each eyebrow is a small hollow—about in the middle.

2. Massage or press one eyebrow at this point for a slow count of 10, release, repeat on the other side for another count of 10. Release, and repeat the process from the beginning, twice more on each side. Lengthy meeting? Repeat as necessary.

* * *

• The phone won't stop ringing, the customers want answers, and you can feel the tension begin to mount. Let your associates drink another cup of coffee or pop a pill. You now have the "handle" to help yourself. This move will reduce the discomfort of a *tension headache* while easing you back into control.

1. On your forehead in the"widow's peak" area is the beginning of this shiatzu point. Place your little finger on this spot and spread your fingers about a half inch apart right along a middle part line.

2. Begin by applying pressure with your little finger, move next to your ring finger, on to your middle finger and then to your index finger. Complete the movement by applying pressure or massaging where your thumb is located on top of your head. Repeat the sequence for one minute.

* * *

• Here's a movement especially designed for **migraines**. If you have "warnings" before the headache strikes this is a good set of shiatzu moves for you to learn. Use them as soon as you realize that you are in for an attack. If you don't recognize any migraine warning signals, try using these moves once (or several) times every day.

1. Between attacks, rub the neck and back as far as you can reach.

2. Apply pressure for a slow count of five to each of the following spots: just below the navel, about four inches below the top of the knee on the outside of the calf, in the web between the index finger and the thumb, and at the midline of the chest between the nipples. Use a counter clockwise motion and repeat the entire sequence, but this time massage your other hand and calf. The treatment will take only about 60 seconds and you can repeat it as often as necessary.

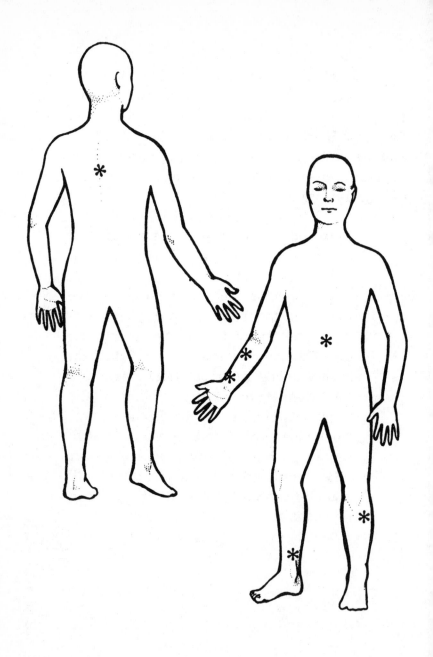

*Location of shiatzu points for Chapter 3 exercises.

3

Abdominal Area

Unless you're into "bathroom humor," abdominal afflictions are no laughing matter. And the simple truth is that you can't work well when your stomach rumbles, growls, and generally feels terrible.

Shiatzu can help encourage smooth digestion, give you relief from constipation, and bring your body back into balance when you have an occasional acidy abdomen. It's sensible and drug free, and you can use it anytime abdominal discomfort strikes.

Be sure to relax before you do each movement. You may find the movements work more effectively in sequence, that is, start with the first and go through each movement. Total time? Less than five minutes. An antacid tablet will take a lot longer than that to work—with shiatzu you do it naturally.

• Does stress kick you in the stomach? Did you eat or drink too much? Try this movement to relieve *abdominal upsets and indigestion*. Many have found it to be extremely effective for tired legs, hemorrhoids, and varicose veins.

1. In a sitting position with feet flat on the floor, slip your left hand into the 90 degree angle of your right leg, with thumb under the bend.

2. Place fingers around the front of your leg and make an imaginary line from the middle finger to a spot on the outside of your calf, about four or five inches from the top of your knee.

3. Massage or apply pressure to this point for 10 seconds, repeat on the left leg. Do each leg three times for maximum revitalization. This is an excellent relaxer after a weekend football match or anytime you want to calm down internally.

* * *

• With many shiatzu movements, you actually get double, sometimes triple benefits from one exercise. This next movement will ***improve digestion, alleviate stomach upset and relieve stiff painful arms*** (from playing one too many games of racquetball or tennis). Try it:

1. Locate the spot on the forearm muscle about an inch and a half from the elbow

crease—on the thumb side of your arm. Using your four fingers, gently apply a circular, massaging pressure on this point.

2. As you massage, don't be afraid to gently separate the muscles with your fingers. Never cause yourself pain, but feel for a "knot" or tight spot while you move the skin and muscles. Continue for a count of twenty-five, release, and repeat for a count of twenty-five on the other arm.

* * *

• No one wants to have that sick, green feeling—especially when there's important business to do. *Nausea* is no fun—yet when you eat too fast, or when you eat and conduct a meeting at the same time, it's no wonder your stomach rebels. Let shiatzu relieve that discomfort without announcing to your associates, superior, or staff that you're not up to par. Use this next movement.

1. On the inside of your forearm, about an inch and a half from the first wrist fold, closest to the palm, is the shiatzu spot you will want to massage.

2. Between the two tendons, massage in a clockwise direction for a count of 10, release, and massage the same way on your other arm. Continue alternating arms and repeat for a total of 60 seconds.

* * *

• This movement may take a bit of practice, but it will *improve digestion and relieve hiccoughs* (which is great news—it's impossible to be taken seriously when you're making hiccoughing noises).

1. With your right arm, reach up in back to locate the tip of your shoulder blade. Make an imaginary line to the middle of your back and massage this point.

2. Massage gently for 20 seconds, release, exhale and inhale deeply, and repeat two more times. (For hiccoughs, you may need to repeat the sequence or ask for assistance in applying pressure to this point.)

* * *

• Isn't *abdominal pain* the last problem you want to deal with when you're working hard and loving it? Yes, even people who routinely use shiatzu will sometimes get the flu or eat something that just doesn't "set" right. But what do they do—what can you do? For relief of occasional stomach upsets, try this next movement which is also suggested for diarrhea and insomnia.

1. Inside your calf, about four finger-widths from the top of your ankle bone is the massage point.

2. Gently rub this area on the right leg for a count of 15, relax, and move to the left leg. After another count of 15, relax for a moment and repeat the process on both legs.

* * *

• To rid yourself of the *feeling that "it's all going to come up"* use this next three-point move:

1. On your forearm about three inches up from the wrist crease, on the inside, is the spot you will massage first. Apply pressure or massage for a slow count of 10, then repeat on the other wrist before doing the next step.

2. Place your fingers about five inches up from the navel. Apply a counter clockwise massage for a slow count of 20, then proceed with step 3.

3. On your right leg, use the fingers of your left hand to massage and apply pressure

to the outside of your calf about four inches down from your knee bend. Continue for a slow count of 10, then repeat on the left leg.

With this movement it's essential to keep your breathing steady, first exhaling deeply, then inhaling from the lowest portion of the lungs.

CHAPTER

4

Shoulders and That Deep Ache Inside

Backache, tightness and tenderness around your neckline? Call it what you like, but if you have it you probably remember how the tightness starts right at your shoulders and spreads out from there. If you can stop it before it completely takes hold, you'll be back in business in one minute flat.

Sample the following moves in the order given. However, once you've tried them, let your body decide what works best. Each is slightly different, but these exercises are just what you want when you're determined to be in control of your total body conditioning.

• Individuals who experience **tenseness in the shoulders**, sometimes refer to the spot where stiffness builds up as the "yipe point." It's possible to relieve that tension now with these two easy steps.

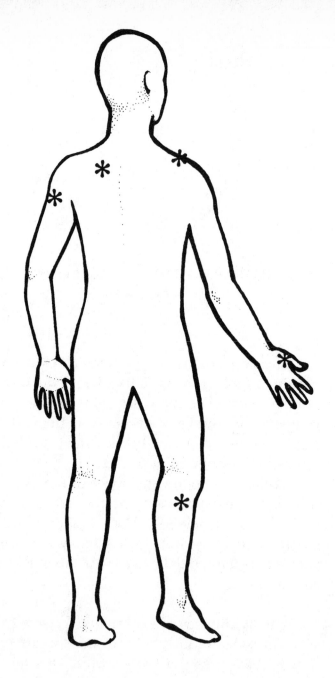

*Location of shiatzu points for Chapter 4 exercises.

1. To locate this shiatzu point, move your right hand across your chest and touch the fleshy shoulder area midway between the base of your neck and the edge of your shoulder. Now move your hand slightly to the rear and feel a depression.

2. Apply a circular massage in this spot for 10 seconds. Relax, and repeat on the other side. Relax, and massage the left side again. Continue the process for 60 seconds. Remember you can't "OD" on shiatzu, so feel free to use it as often as necessary.

* * *

• In some future world every executive might have a relaxation laser with which to apply light to the body for total relief of **tension.** In this "now" time, allow shiatzu to increase your personal effectiveness in **any** situation. With this movement, you must reach further across your back to apply shiatzu massage to the areas which become extra tender when you must sit for long periods of time.

1. Extend your left hand over your right shoulder (or behind your head) and reach as far as possible. Massage and apply pressure from the lowest point you can reach up to the top of your shoulder.

Don't panic if you can't reach very far, just massage as much of the area as possible.

2. Massage in four or five spots in this area. Repeat four times on that side, then repeat the moves on the left shoulder/back area.

* * *

• If your sensitivity occurs in the **upper portion of the body**, use this shiatzu move which is especially designed to loosen and re-activate the arms and shoulders. With one session—one minute's time—you'll renew energy and relieve soreness, instantly making movement easier.

1. Place your thumb under your armpit, and your index and middle fingers on top of your arm. Apply pressure or massage to the top of your arm for a slow count of 10, then move your fingers down your arm slightly and massage again for a count of 10. Next, place your index and middle fingers in the hollow under the outer part of your collarbone. Massage for a count of 10.

2. Now repeat the entire sequence on your other side. Remember to breath deeply and consciously relax those muscles.

* * *

• Relax and relieve **tightness in the shoulder joint** with this simple movement. Do it slowly and feel your fingertips healing the area.

1. Extend right arm straight out from the shoulder with thumb pointing up. With your left hand, touch the top of the shoulder and locate a small indentation.

2. Massage this area for 30 seconds before moving to the left side, where the procedure is repeated.

* * *

• Pain is the body's way of signaling that something's amiss. Use it as a barometer of your health, and use this next movement for **general stiffness** in the upper portion of the body.

1. Apply pressure or pulsating massage to the web between the thumb and index finger on your right hand, using the thumb and index finger of your left. Continue for a slow count of 15, and repeat on the other hand.

2. Place your left hand on the outside of your left calf, about four inches down from the top of your knee. With your fingers apply a counter clockwise

massage to this point for a slow count of 15, relax for a moment and repeat on the right leg using the right hand.

When you become attuned to your body—really listening to the energy flowing inside—you may discover there are other points which would benefit from *60-Second Shiatzu*. Use these techniques at those points to bring relief. Use light stroking, deeper touching, circular pressure, or other gentle movements you can create yourself. Experiment, and decide what feels good to you.

✳ ✳ ✳

CHAPTER

5

Lower Intestinal Aches

Picture this—you're sitting in the corporate office, subordinates are circling the table, and you're suddenly hit by a stabbing gas pain and feel your spine go rigid. Not pleasant, right? But there's nothing to do about it? Wrong!

Tension builds up in the lower abdominal area from excessive gas, sensitivity to foods, or the flu, among other causes. No one is immune, but now that you understand the concepts of shiatzu, you have a choice. Why suffer when you can relieve the discomfort with shiatzu? (However, be health smart, and if fever, severe pain, or vomiting accompanies any of the symptoms above, do your body a favor and do not perform any shiatzu before you consult a medical professional.)

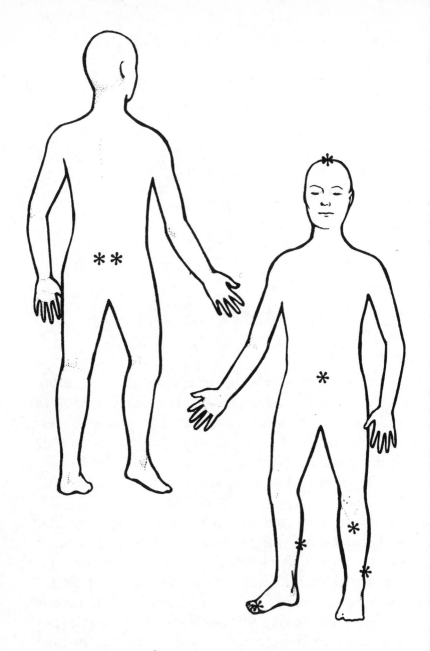

*Location of shiatzu points for Chapter 5 exercises.

• Sometimes the foods you most enjoy will rebel in your intestines. At times, there's no reason for it except that you ate too fast or had too much of a good thing. To relieve that *"too full" feeling* quickly, do this simple shiatzu movement.

1. In a sitting position, reach down and place your fingers on your leg about four inches above your ankle bone on the outside area of your calf. Your little finger should be closest to your ankle bone. In the spot where your index finger lies is the shiatzu massage point. Begin on the left leg with your left hand.

2. Massage this spot for a slow count of 10, relax, and repeat on the right side. Repeat the entire sequence, 10 counts on each side, for a total of 60 seconds.

* * *

• As an active, success-oriented individual, *diarrhea* may be the result of plain old excitement or it may be caused by a simple upset stomach or the flu. Whatever the cause, treat it quickly and without swallowing a pill. This next movement is specifically designed to help relieve the problem, putting you back in action fast. (Of course, for severe diarrhea, consult your physician.)

As the marvels of shiatzu spread through ancient Japan, it was rumored that this movement was used in the treatment of cholera, but don't save it until you feel that disease coming on. Just use it the next time you're feeling queasy.

1. In a sitting position, place your left thumb under your left knee slightly to the outside of the shin bone. Measure down four fingers to the massage spot.

2. Apply pressure or massage to this area for a count of 25, relax, exhale deeply, then breathe in through your mouth, first filling the lowest portion of your lungs. Repeat the procedure on your right leg.

* * *

• *Constipation* is almost predictable when you're traveling and out of your normal routine. Suffer no more—treat yourself with Shiatzu. This next procedure is excellent for occasional constipation and it's said to improve digestion and bowel functions. Develop a habit of performing this movement the first thing in the morning—every day, whether you're at home or away. Many have beat constipation by using this shiatzu movement and by drinking a hot liquid just before beginning the routine. Be sure to keep the fiber high in your diet regardless of where you roam.

1. While sitting, locate the area on the back of your calf about midway between the crease at your knee and the top of your ankle.

2. Rub and press in this area, starting with the left leg, using your left hand. Use a circular movement and make your touch as soft or hard as is comfortable. Relax for a moment and repeat on the right calf. Use shiatzu on each leg for about 30 seconds.

* * *

• ***Constipation*** is a common and contemporary complaint. To restore balance to the lower intestinal area, increase the fiber in your diet and consume more liquids. Before you resort to taking another pill, use this movement. Many have found that this treatment and the one above work extremely well in combination.

1. Using your left thumb or index finger, massage the lower portion of your right big toe nail on the inside corner (that is, the spot closest to the second toe, but on the nail itself). You may find this is easier to do if your other hand is supporting the foot.

2. Apply a circle pressure with the index finger for a count of 25, relax, and repeat on the left toe nail.

* * *

• To promote healthy *intestinal functions* should be your goal. Use this next movement to smooth out those digestive ripples that hit every once in a while, or use it on a regular basis as a preventive measure.

1. Place your fingertips on your hip bones at your sides and extend your thumbs to the back muscles.

2. With the thumbs, massage and press down toward your feet for a count of 25, relax, and repeat the same movement for another count of 25.

* * *

• *Hemorrhoids* are part of life for a high percentage of Americans. Why—the theory goes that we're a nation of fast food lovers and don't get enough fiber. Here's a three minute medication alternative. This shiatzu move will help relieve the pressure and pain of hemorrhoids. Use it daily, but also give your body a chance to heal itself by including plenty of citrus foods, naturally fibrous foods, and whole grains in your diet.

1. Place your left hand two inches below the navel at the center line of the body. Rub, apply pulsating pressure or clock-

wise massage on this point for a slow
count of 30, relax, and repeat.

2. Locate the slight depression on the very
    top of the head. Using your left hand,
    apply a pulsating massage for a slow
    count of 30, relax, exhale, inhale, and
    repeat for another count of 30.

3. With your left hand, place your fingers
    on the back of your left calf about mid-
    way between the back knee crease and
    the top of your ankle. Apply a clockwise
    massage for a slow count of 30, relax, and
    repeat on the right calf.

* * *

If you choose to do a total energizing shiatzu
treatment each morning, be sure to include one of
the moves in this chapter. If stress often hits you in
the belly, make one of these movements a part of your
morning routine and use it before each meal. Your
health will be better for it.

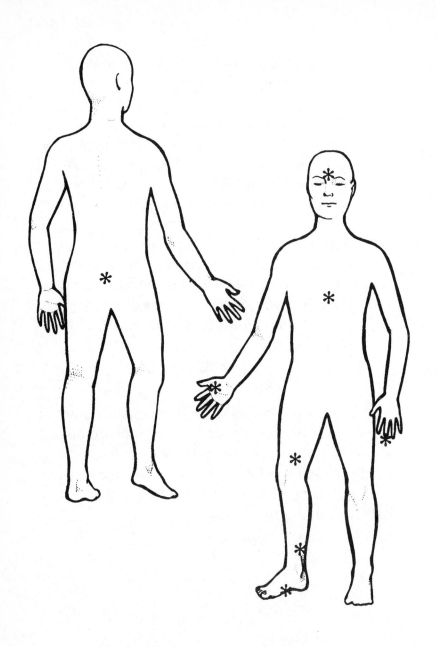

✱ Location of shiatzu points for Chapter 6 exercises.

CHAPTER

6

Menstrual Pains and PMS

For relief from menstrual pains and PMS, you can't beat the drug-free relief you can get with shiatzu. If you chronically suffer, incorporate one or two of these moves into your morning energizing plan—do it every day, and within a month's time you should notice improvement. Be sure to discuss your treatment with your doctor—maybe she'd profit from shiatzu, too.

Keep the instructions for these moves at hand—you may want to do them routinely during the mid-cycle days, before your period, and to ease any discomfort during your period. Remember, shiatzu is totally natural and you should experience relief almost instantly. Before you resort to medication, give your body the TLC it deserves.

For women only? As a supportive male, don't skip this chapter. Instead, review the shiatzu moves with your spouse, lover, girlfriend, or mother.

Before doing these moves, exhale and inhale deeply, and rub your hands together fast enough to feel the energy between your palms. Allow that warmth to flow through your fingers into your body. Begin with the first move, but do try them all because each has a slightly different result and only you will know what works best.

• Tension, anxiety, and a feeling that the world is "out to get you" is currently known as *PMS* (pre-menstrual syndrome). Try this move to relieve that anguish and bring your life back into balance.

1. Locate the middle point between your eyebrows, directly above the bridge of your nose.

2. Apply circular massage for a slow count of 30, exhale and inhale deeply, then repeat. For an added feeling of relief, close your eyes during this movement and listen to your breathing while zeroing in on your heartbeat. Repeat as often as necessary. You may find a smooth, stroking, or pulsating massage works more effectively—experiment enough to find which works best for you.

* * *

• Suddenly without any warning, you feel your mouth begin to turn down, or your shoulders cramp, or just a dizzy, cloudy feeling forms around your brain. Regardless of what your appointment book says, it could be PMS intruding into your day. If you have this problem, you already know that **PMS** happens at the worst possible times—usually when you're crucially involved.

You definitely don't want to ''advertise'' the fact that you're not bursting with energy—that would be bad for your business image—instead, try this shiatzu move that's so subtle no one will be wiser, but you, as your mood begins to change in 60 seconds.

1. Locate this shiatzu point on your middle finger on the thumb-side in the lower fingernail area of your right hand.

2. Using your left index finger or thumb, press or massage the spot for a count of 15, then switch to the left hand for a count of 15 before repeating this entire sequence.

* * *

• *Menstrual pain* can be relieved at your desk, or even at the conference table, with this simple move. If possible take three deep breaths, first exhaling deeply, then inhaling in a slow, measured way, first filling your lower lungs.

1. While sitting, put the fingers of your left hand about three inches above your knee on the inside of your left thigh.

2. Massage, stroke, and apply gentle, circular pressure to this area for a count of 15, then treat your right leg in the same way. Repeat the movement again from right to left, counting a slow 15 each time.

* * *

• If you work in a private office, there's no problem relieving *menstrual discomfort* with this next move. Out in the open or in a glassed-in office? Simply locate a private corner and treat yourself to health.

1. Take off your shoes and cross your right leg over your left knee with the foreleg parallel to the floor. On the bottom of your foot, locate the small depression behind the ball of the foot. Now move your left thumb one inch toward your arch.

2. Massage and apply pressure to this area for a count of 30, relax, and repeat on the left foot.

• *Cramps* are one "benefit" of womanhood you can easily do without. Don't allow monthly pains to get you down—it's bad for your image and has negative impact on your career. Instead try this three-point movement, and for even better results, supplement shiatzu with an exercise program such as walking, swimming, or non-percussive aerobic dance.

1. Apply pressure or massage to:
   A. The web between your thumb and index finger,
   B. About four inches above your ankle bone on the inside of your calf,
   C. The fleshy spot about three inches above your knee bend, on the inside of your calf.

2. Using the left hand, do all three movements on the right side of your body for a count of 10 each, then repeat the complete sequence on the left side. You can do the entire routine as many times as necessary to relax and relieve the distress of cramping and PMS.

* * *

• To relieve *bloating*, just before your period or during PMS days, try this next shiatzu combination. Yes, it takes more than 60 seconds, but isn't your body worth it?

1. Using your left hand, gently apply a pulsating pressure halfway between your collarbone and your navel and continue for a slow count of 30, relax, and move on to step two.

2. Place the fingers of your left hand four inches up from your ankle bone on your left inside calf. Apply counter clockwise massage for a slow count of 30, relax, and repeat on the right leg. This exercise should be done while sitting, and may be easier if you reach around to the shiatzu spot from the back of your leg.

3. In a standing position or lying on your stomach, place the fingers of your left hand on your spine, at the spot commonly called the "tail bone." Massage, stroke, or apply pressure to this shiatzu point for a slow count of 30. Relax, exhale, and inhale deeply. Repeat for another count of 30.

* * *

Don't hesitate to repeat the entire sequence, and if you're a woman prone to swelling, make this last combination of moves a regular part of your morning routine.

CHAPTER

7

Insomnia

There's no chance for a person like you to be accused of sleeping on the job. On the contrary, you're determined to give it all you've got "200%" of the time. But aren't there nights when you carry home career-related conflicts and a heavy work schedule inside that bulging brief case? Insomnia is the end result. Don't pop another pill when you can switch to the safe and sane alternative to sleepless hours—*60-Second Shiatzu.* Here are five of the best movements. You may want to do them in a series or concentrate your effort using a favorite. Keep this chapter open on your night stand for easy reference when the "sandman" turns down your invitation.

As strange as it sounds, the reason most people can't sleep is because they don't think they can! It's true, one of the best methods to bring on sleep is by making bedtime as routine as possible. Sleep authorities suggest that you keep the bedroom strictly for sleep and sex, but once you realize the powers of shiatzu, you'll want to add it to the other two"S's."

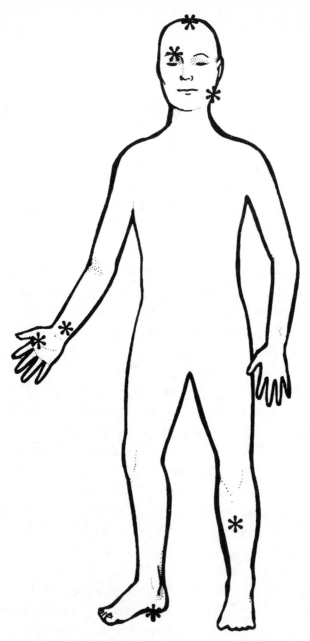

*Location of shiatzu points for Chapter 7 exercises.

Without knowing it, you may be undermining your nights—by eating too late or by watching the nightly news. If after a few nights of using one or all of these moves you're still unable to sleep, look for deeper problems and don't hesitate to discuss your concerns with a professional.

Become familiar with these moves, but also incorporate moves from other chapters, including shiatzu for headaches, stomach upsets, or backaches. Remember, there could be other reasons for being unable to locate the sandman, and they may have nothing at all to do with a stressful lifestyle—for example, your shoulders and neck muscles can get just as tense from a long tennis match or a vigorous hour's swim as from sitting all day in a business meeting or at a computer keyboard. Shiatzu will still relieve the tenseness, but the effectiveness of the treatments may be enhanced if you combine your shiatzu routines with other relaxation techniques.

For a night of sound, restful sleep, perhaps you'd like to try one or all of the following suggestions in conjunction with shiatzu. Take a hot bath before bed, practice some very mild yoga or stretching, and if you have a snack, make it a food high in calcium, such as yogurt, cheese, or milk. You should sleep like a baby.

• If you're keyed up and the hour's late, try this movement about ten minutes before bed, then repeat it when you crawl between the covers. Sleep well!

1. In a sitting position, place the index and middle fingers of each hand on the crown of your head. Spread the fingers slightly.

2. Using all your fingers, apply pressure or massage for a count of 15, release, allow your head to come forward onto your chest, take a breath, and repeat from the beginning. Continue the movement for 60 seconds.

* * *

• Just know you won't sleep? Exhale deeply and feel the oxygen fill your lungs as you inhale, starting from the lowest portion. Close your eyes, and continue to breathe deeply for a few minutes. Then to relax and release *tension*, try this next shiatzu movement.

1. Place your thumbs or index fingers near the center of your eyebrows. Feel around a bit until you locate a small depression.

2. Apply a circular, slightly pressured massage to these spots for a slow count of 10, relax, and repeat five more times. Be sure to close your eyes during this movement and breathe deeply.

* * *

• This shiatzu move is excellent whenever you feel the ***need to relax***—in a taxi between mad-dash appointments or when you're scheduled far over your head. For quick relief take a moment for this shiatzu movement. It's designed for those nights when sleep escapes you, but use it anytime you need to catch your breath and truly relax.

1. These shiatzu points are about two finger widths below your earlobes under the edge of the jaw on your neck.

2. Use a gentle pressure, a pulsating touch, or a counter clockwise massage on these points for a slow count of 15, relax, and repeat for a total of four times.

* * *

• You're giving the treatment and you know your body. Make the pressure of this next movement comfortable to you—some enjoy a light touch while others feel shiatzu is more effective with firmer pressure.

Try this move about 20 minutes before bed to encourage ***natural sleep***, then repeat it while lying in bed with your eyes closed. Make shiatzu a routine part of bedtime, and if it would be useful, memorize two or three of the moves in this chapter to help lull you to dreamland.

1. Locate the point on the inside of your right wrist, between the tendons.

2. Begin on your right arm with your left thumb and index finger. Apply a pinching, massaging movement for a count of 15, then repeat the treatment on the left arm with your right thumb and index finger. Relax for a moment and repeat the entire sequence.

* * *

• Really convince yourself that you can and will *sleep*. Even say outloud, "This shiatzu move relaxes me and helps me sleep."

Where do you feel the tension when you can't sleep? If tight neck muscles and stiffness in the shoulder area compound sleeplessness, use the movements outlined in Chapter 4, along with this next movement, to completely remove the word "insomnia" from your memory bank.

1. Lying in bed or sitting on the edge, place your lower right leg across your left knee. Take the sole of your foot into your left hand and press the area just in front of your heel pad for 15 seconds.

2. Work with your thumbs up an imaginary line to the middle toe with a circular massage. Repeat this sequence on your other foot. You may want to do this movement again or with some of the other exercises in this chapter for maximum benefits.

• Here's a two-part move that takes more than 60 seconds, but will relax you and ***allow you to rest***. Commit it to memory if you must travel and want to spend your nights sleeping instead of rumpling the covers. It'll let you get to that early AM meeting bright eyed and bursting with vigor.

1. Using your left hand, place the thumb and index finger on the web between the thumb and index finger of your right hand. Apply a pulsating pressure or counter clockwise massage to this spot for a slow count of 30. Relax and repeat on the left hand, then go to step two.

2. In a sitting position, bend forward and place the fingers of your left hand on your left front calf, about halfway between the knee and the front of your ankle (the shin). Stroke up and down or apply a pressured, circular massage to this area of the left calf for a slow count of 30. Relax, exhale, inhale, and repeat on the right calf in the same shiatzu spot.

3. Lie back, close your eyes and count backward from 60. Repeat as necessary.

Make shiatzu a habit as you help yourself to natural, drug-free sleep.

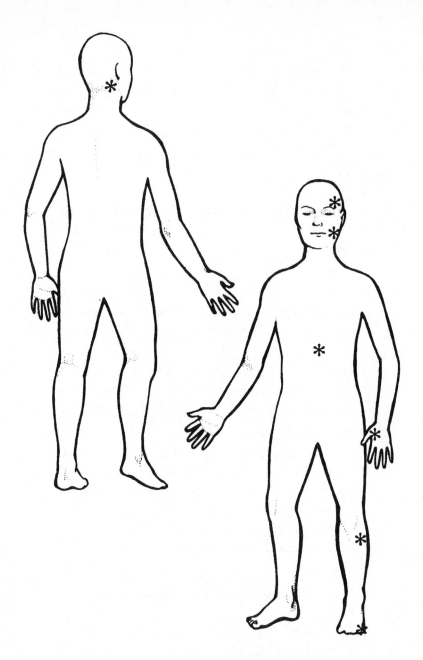

∗ Location of shiatzu points for Chapter 8 exercises.

8

Loosening That Tight Jaw

The day's schedule has been murder, your secretary is out with the flu, and the annual audit is dangerously close. Your jaw automatically clenches tighter with each interruption; every phone call results in more tension.

This is the perfect time to use shiatzu to help you regain your quick and intuitive business sense. Use the exercises in this chapter when your world is chaotic and you'll be back in charge almost instantly.

Since stress hits each of us in a different spot, and that tight jaw may be just part of the problem—your head may ache, and your shoulders probably feel tense, too. Make shiatzu a part of your life and treat that jaw tension, but also select moves from other chapters to treat tension in your head, shoulders, and back.

• Get rid of *stress* now. You needn't tell the world you're under pressure because now you have the "handle" to relieve your tension with this subtle movement.

1. Just above and slightly forward from your ear on your temple (about one inch above the top rim of your ear toward your nose), is the shiatzu point you'll want to locate. Touch the area with your fingertips. If your jaw is as tight as a spring, you may experience a tenderness here, so begin your massage with a very gentle touch.

2. Apply a circular massage or pressure to both sides of your head with your index finger or thumb for a count of 15, relax, repeat three more times. By exhaling deeply while you're doing this move, you'll also be releasing built-up tension.

* * *

• You can easily do this next move anywhere, anytime, to cure your *aching jaw*. Be sure to exhale deeply, follow with a deep inhalation beginning at the lowest portions of your lungs. If possible, close your eyes once you've reviewed the instructions and begin the exercise.

1. To find the massage point, first put a finger on your hair line at the back of your head above your spine. Directly be-

tween this point and the spot where your earlobe joins your face is the area to be massaged. You may want to massage in a triangle and use the movement in three places. Begin with this move and then personalize it to fit your needs.

2. Massage in a circular motion or apply pressure on each side of your head simultaneously for a count of 15, relax, and repeat this massage three more times. Remember, exhale deeply, then inhale as if you're breathing in mountain air on a spring afternoon.

* * *

• This movement is more obvious and could capture the attention of business associates, but it's a great way to get relief when your *jaw is too tight to talk*. It is best done while seated, either bending over or with your foreleg across your knee. If you decide to do it while in a business meeting, don't be surprised if you're asked for your other shiatzu secrets after you explain this one.

1. Remove your shoes. Locate the shiatzu point on the little toe between the toe knuckle and the nail.

2. Rub your hands together briskly. Using your left hand, apply a pinching pressure or massage to this spot. Hold and pinch for a slow count of 30, release, rub your hands together again, and repeat the move on the other foot for a count of 30.

* * *

• With some shiatzu movements, you apply the massage on an energy line (meridian) to bring relief to a totally different part of the body. With this move you'll apply pressure or massage directly to the *tight jaw* area. There's a possibility that you may experience some sensitivity, therefore, keep in mind that the more tender an area is the more tension you will need to work out. Do go lightly when you begin, and repeat as necessary throughout the day.

2. Rub your hands together as if warming them on a chilly morning, then run your fingers over the outer edge of your jaw, starting at your ear. You want to locate a slight depression in the jaw line about one inch from the beginning of the jaw bone under the ear.

2. Treating both sides of your jaw at the same time, place your thumbs or index fingers in the indentations and apply circular pressure for a slow count of 10, relax for a moment, and repeat four more

times. Some individuals find continuing
the circular pressure down their entire
jawline to the chin brings faster relief.

* * *

• Use one or more of the last four moves, then
try this treatment to *revitalize your mind and
body:*

1. Using the fingers of our left hand, apply
   a pulsating or clockwise massage to the
   midpoint between your collarbone and
   navel, in the area called "the pit" of the
   stomach. Do so for a slow count of 30,
   relax, exhale and inhale, then repeat for
   another count of 30.

2. With your left thumb and index finger
   apply massage or a firm pressure on the
   web between the index finger and thumb
   of the right hand, for a slow count of 30.
   Relax, and repeat on the left hand.

3. Finish this shiatzu movement by applying clockwise massage or pressure to the
   point about four inches below the knee
   on the outside of the calf. Begin with the
   left hand on the left leg for a slow count
   of 30, relax for a moment, and repeat on
   the right leg.

* * *

When using these natural methods to energize and relax, do keep in mind that you must always listen to your body first. Although your primary goal may be to treat and relax the tension in your jaw, it's probably built up in your shoulder and neck as well. After you've relaxed your jaw, go directly to the chapters on treating other parts of the body. To Chapter 2, for instance, to relieve head and neck pain, or to Chapter 6, if you're suffering from PMS. Make shiatzu work for you.

For a really dynamite system, how about adding a **super energizer**, from Chapter 14, to the moves you've already mastered? You know shiatzu can relieve your headache and control an upset stomach, so what's stopping you from treating yourself to an entire revitalizing routine? Take the time **now**—you'll be glad you did.

CHAPTER

9

Backache Begone

Is the problem your chair, that ancient mattress, or your dynamite backswing? It could be too much too fast in a weekend sport or it could be stress—plain and simple—that's making your back ache. Whatever the cause, when backache strikes what you want most is prompt and drug-free relief. That's exactly where the power of your own touch enters the picture. Use shiatzu along with other common sense treatments. If you have a chronic problem, you need to seek out professional advice, but for occasional relief or to enhance your doctor's program, shiatzu is the answer.

• *Backaches* are as common a complaint as headaches and they actually take more people to the doctor than colds or the flu. If you've never suffered back problems, you may find it hard to imagine the depth of this kind of discomfort—but don't skip this chapter because you "know" you'll never need it. The next time you smash a tennis ball or pick up your

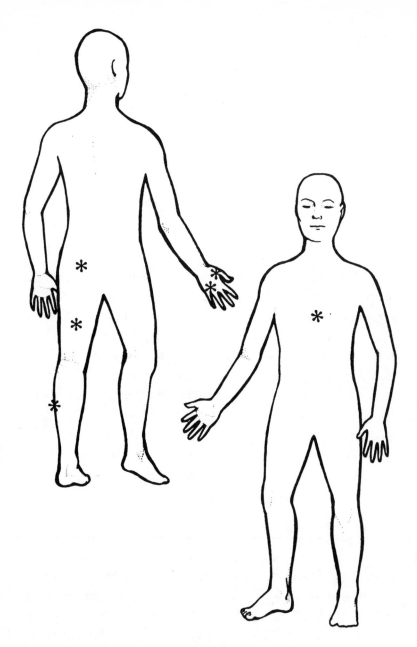

*Location of shiatzu points for Chapter 9 exercises.

niece, you could feel a twinge that will turn into a backache. So give this chapter the once over, know that the information on shiatzu is available to you whenever you need it, and if the opportunity arises, share it with a friend.

Incorporate a smooth, stretching program into your regular fitness routine to help condition the muscles of your back. Give your abdominal muscles the once over, too—many backaches are aggravated by protruding tummy muscles or poor posture. But should backache strike—go ahead and treat your next pain in the spine with this movement.

1. Find the spot on the back of your hand where the ring finger and the little finger long bones meet—called the fourth and fifth metacarpals. You may need to "feel around" to locate the area. Use your left hand to apply pulsating or clockwise pressure to this spot. No need to press hard, but allow your fingers to search out the right spot.

2. Massage or apply gentle pressure to this point on the right hand for a slow count of 10, repeat the procedure on the left hand. Continue alternating hands and massage for a total of 60 seconds.

* * *

• With shiatzu, it's always up to you to decide how much pressure to apply. There's a very slim line between pleasure and pain—if you're unsure as to how much pressure will be most effective, apply a stroking touch, repeat with a firm massage, and if you feel more is better, allow your fingers to press into your body.

Your own gentle touch really can help relieve your **back pain** when you use this movement. Stand up with feet about 12 inches apart. Take a few deep breaths, exhaling deeply, then inhaling, filling the lowest portion of your lungs first. Pretend you're inhaling brisk, winter air and really breathe your fill.

1. Run the fingers of your left hand down the back of your thigh. You're looking for the energy point located between the soft spot above the knee and the fold of your buttocks, the spot where the muscles divide. Finding this spot will be much easier if you have access to a full length mirror.

2. Apply pressure or massage at this natural division in the muscles for a count of 30, relax for a moment, and repeat for another count of 30. You may want to do each leg individually or both at the same time. Do the moves that feel right—and you'll be right on.

* * *

• To reduce *muscle spasm* caused from over-action or a chronic back problem and reduce the pain in your back, so you can function normally—pain free again, do this simple shiatzu move. First exhale deeply, wait for a second, then inhale deeply starting at the lowest portion of your lungs.

1. In a sitting position, find this shiatzu point half way between the crease at the back of your knee and the top of your ankle. You'll find a spot where the muscles divide.

2. Apply pressure or massage to this area on both legs for a slow count of 30, relax, exhale deeply, and inhale starting from the lower portion of your lungs, before you begin the sequence again.

* * *

• *Sciatica* is more than a fancy name for a backache, and if you've ever experienced its peculiar torture you know it's truly a pain in the butt. To help relieve this distress, use the moves in the last exercise and complete the treatment with this one. Once your back pain has been relieved, you may discover that you're ready to treat the stiffness in your shoulders or the queasy feeling in your stomach that sometimes accompanies a sciatica attack. You know your body best, treat it with care. Use any of the other exercises that are appropriate.

1. Standing up or lying on your stomach, locate this shiatzu spot on the side of the buttocks, about three inches from your spine.

2. You may want to start with a light massage, and switch to a deeper, pressured massage as the muscles begin to relax. Continue massage for at least a count of 30 on each side. Repeat as needed.

* * *

• To relieve *all-over stiffness* and to use in conjunction with the shiatzu backache remedies already described, try this one:

1. Using the fingers of your left hand, apply a counter clockwise pressure massage to the point on your chest, midway between your collarbone and navel. Continue for a slow count of 30, relax and repeat.

2. With the thumb and index finger of your left hand, apply a pulsating pressure massage to the fleshy area of the web between the thumb and index finger of your right hand. Don't be surprised if you discover tenderness—that means you have more tension than you realized, but

shiatzu will help work it out. Massage this spot for a count of 30, relax, repeat on the left hand before going on to step 3.

3. Place the fingers of your left hand about four inches down from the knee bend on the outside of the left calf. Apply a firm pressure to the spot for a slow count of 30, relax, repeat on the right calf.

Remember that once the acute pain of your backache is relieved, the next step is to try moves from other chapters, such as Chapter 12's "Relaxing Moves," to put you back "in the pink."

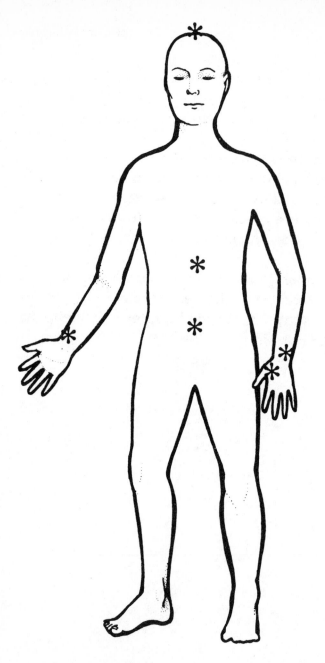

*Location of shiatzu points for Chapter 10 exercises.

CHAPTER

10

Relieving Depression

It's almost inhuman not to experience a bout with the blues from time to time—they can sneak into anyone's life. And when that happens, it's the perfect time to counter the negative feelings with the positive effect of shiatzu. That's right—at your own fingertips, you have a quick and effective mood enhancing alternative.

To relieve simple depression and to give you "handles" should it creep in, even if you've never been a bit "down in the dumps" ever, review these moves and remember that they're available when you need them.

For maximum health, and as a mood elevator, make the right moves for your total body. By combining shiatzu with an aerobic exercise routine and nutritious low-cal food choices, you can truly drop the non-prescription drugs down the drain. Here's your personal invitation to take the responsible approach to the blues. Switch to shiatzu.

If your low moods persist, occur frequently, or are associated with thoughts of suicide, head for the nearest mental health center. Medical intervention may be indicated.

• To cure those occasional blue moods, use this exercise. Exhale deeply, then inhale beginning in the lower portion of your lungs. Close your eyes and pretend you're at the seashore breathing in the fresh, salty air. Continue this way for a moment or two before you begin this movement.

1. Close your eyes as you sit comfortably or lie down. With your left thumb on the inside of your wrist and your fingers on the outside, gently massage the folds on your wrist which are closest to the palm.

2. Begin with a counter clockwise massage, then switch to a clockwise motion. Work on the right wrist in this way for a slow count of 30, about a half minute, before repeating it on the left.

* * *

• This next movement is almost too good to be true—it's fast and relaxes as it rejuvenates even the flattest outlook on life. To really boost the *mood elevating* power, don't hesitate to combine this movement with the last one or others in *60-Second*

Shiatzu. This is your book—write in it, memorize the moves if you like, but use it.

1. Begin by rubbing your hands together as if warming them on a chilly morning. Then place the fingers of your left hand into the hollow above your stomach between the navel and the base of your ribs—along the center line of your upper torso. Spread your fingers slightly if necessary to cover this area.

2. Close your eyes, apply a firm but gentle amount of pressure, and count backwards from 30 to zero, relax, exhale and inhale deeply, then repeat the procedure. You can do the movement lying down or sitting quietly at your desk.

* * *

• Depending on your associates or the group you're with, you may decide it would be better to use this move in privacy because it's a "looker". If necessary, sneak away to the washroom or shut your office door. But regardless of how it looks to others, it works extremely well as a ***mood booster*** when you're feeling down. With shiatzu, you don't have to worry about side-effects as you would with drugs, and the only "over-dosing" effect possible is that of your becoming addicted to this healthful alternative. Now try this movement.

1. Touch the top of your ear. Now think of an imaginary line going straight to the top of your head. Run your finger up the side of your head if necessary to get the correct alignment.

2. Place your left index finger on this spot at the top of your head and apply pressure or massage for a count of 15. Relax, exhale deeply, stop for a moment, then inhale deeply beginning at the lowest portion of your lungs. Repeat the entire sequence knowing relief is on the way. Continue for a total of 60 seconds. It may help to close your eyes and concentrate on the most positive memory you can call up. Hold that thought while you're doing this movement.

* * *

• Once the blue mood lifts, through use of the following movement and the ones preceeding it, take time to physically work out the problem through exercise or other positive actions and conversation.

Share these *mood enhancers* with family, friends, and all those out in the "corporate jungle." Keep in mind that your kids can get down at times, too—remember what it was like to be a teenager? Give them the same alternative to mood-changing drugs.

1. Place your left index finger about an inch below the navel on the midline of your body.

2. Apply pressure or massage in a clockwise motion for 30 seconds, relax, and repeat the movement for a total of 60 seconds. (It's said that to energize you should massage with a clockwise motion, but to relax, make the motion counter-clockwise. As you may have already noticed in other moves, *60-Second Shiatzu* takes advantage of this principle.)

* * *

• Are you feeling down because your *body aches*? To energize all over, review the moves in Chapter 14. Relieve stress with this move that you can do anywhere and anytime. Yes, it takes more than 60 seconds to do this exercise, but you'll be glad you did it.

1. Using your left hand, place your thumb and index finger on the web between the thumb and index finger of your right hand. Apply a pinching or pulsating pressure for a slow count of 30, relax, exhale and inhale deeply, repeat on the left hand. Then go to step 2.

2. Place the fingers of your left hand on the top of your head and apply a clockwise massage to this shiatzu spot for a slow count of 30, relax, exhale and inhale deeply, repeat for another count of 30.

3. Locate the next point on the right wrist about one inch from the outer edge on the little finger side of your hand on the inside of your forearm. Using your left thumb and index finger, pinch or massage for a count of 15, relax for a moment, and switch to the left arm. Repeat the massage for a slow count of 15, relax, and massage each wrist again.

Don't be alarmed if you have a tenderness in any area. It simply means you need to work out the stress with shiatzu. Go gently, and as the tension diminishes, you'll be able to apply more pressure.

11

Shiatzu for Sniffles

They start with a tingle in the nose, next comes the scratchy feeling in your throat, then other parts of your body signal that a germ has by-passed your best defenses.

Summer, winter, fall or spring, those nasty, nose-dripping, cold symptoms can be alleviated with shiatzu. It's just nineties common sense to drink plenty of liquids, get lots of rest, and fill your menus with choices that are high in vitamin C. To further increase your heal-ability, be sure to include shiatzu with the resting part of that prescription. Isn't it a relief to know you can do more than just cope—that you can relieve your ills a drug-free way?

• You may have used this movement to relieve a nagging headache. It works equally well to relieve the *stuffiness* of a cold and the head-pounding pain that can accompany those germs.

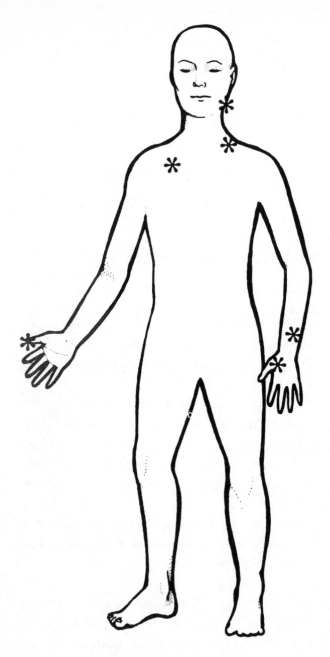

*Location of shiatzu points for Chapter 11 exercises.

1. Place the thumb and index finger of your right hand on opposite sides of the "web" between the thumb and index finger of your left hand.

2. Use a pinching massage to this spot for 30 seconds, then repeat on the right hand using the same technique.

* * *

• Where do the symptoms congregate in your body? If they go directly to your chest without passing "go," here's the right shiatzu move for your next cold. To improve lung capacity and relieve cough and **cold symptoms**, try this movement along with the advice from your physician.

1. Place your fingers on the hollow directly beneath your collarbone. To find this point easily, bring your shoulder forward, and slip your fingers, into the indentation between your collarbone and shoulder.

2. Begin on your right shoulder, using the fingers of your left hand to apply circular pressure. Massage for 15 seconds (or a slow count of 15), then repeat on the left side. Repeat the entire sequence—both right and left sides—for a period of one minute. Try to exhale all the oxygen in

your lungs as you're doing this movement. When you do inhale, fill your chest
cavity from the lower portion up, expand-
ing as you go. It may help to raise your
chin as you inhale, then exhale from your
mouth.

* * *

• At the first sign of those discomforting, yet
familiar, *cold symptoms* sneaking in, use this next
movement. It works especially well when done along
with the others in this section and the relaxing moves
from Chapter 12.

1. Place your right hand on a table, palm
   down. Spread your fingers in a fan. Now
   with the fingers of your left hand
   measure three finger's distance from the
   crease on the top of your wrist toward
   your elbow.

2. Massage for a count of 15, relax, repeat
   for another count of 15. Do this same
   sequence on the left wrist for a total of
   60 seconds of shiatzu. Keep your touch
   gentle unless you enjoy a firmer massage.
   A circular action—clockwise, works well
   for most individuals, and you can repeat
   the entire movement anytime during the
   day.

* * *

• This point may take a moment's practice to find, but it's well worth it when you're ***riddled with cold germs*** and want to eradicate the symptoms NOW.

1. Locate the fleshy spot midway between the end of your shoulder and the point where your neck joins your trunk. Rub your hands together briskly before you begin the movement. Now extend your left arm across your chest and touch the massage spot on the top of your shoulder with the tips of your fingers.

2. Massage or apply pressure to this area for a count of 15, relax, repeat on the left side using your right hand. Repeat the entire procedure for a total of 60 seconds. If this area feels sensitive, it's probably from tension related to the cold. This is also an excellent movement when you need to relieve the shoulder aches that can accompany the sniffles. Don't be afraid to take it a step further and massage the entire area on top of your shoulder with gentle, soothing strokes.

* * *

• ***Sore throat*** can be an instant indicator that something is seriously amiss with your body, but for the simple sore throats which signal a cold, try this next movement. This time you'll massage on a pressure point to help relieve the soreness of your throat. Here's all you have to do:

1. Locate the point on your right thumb at the lower portion of your thumb nail closest to your index finger.

2. Now massage or apply pressure to this spot for 15 seconds, switch to the left hand and repeat the movement. If you have a sore throat only on one side, press the point on that side only. For example, if you only have discomfort on the left side of your throat, you'll massage the left thumbnail area. Continue the movement for a total of 60 seconds.

***

• Bring your body back into balance with this movement which you may want to use just before bed—it can totally relax you, and that's important news if the *sniffles* bring you sleepless hours.

1. From the tips of your earlobes measure down about the width of two fingers onto your neck.

2. Use a gentle, counter clockwise massage or pulsating touch for a slow count of 30,

relax, and repeat. Remember, the relaxing power is in your own touch, so don't hesitate to continue with a gentle massage until you experience relief. If there's tenderness, it only means you must begin very lightly and apply a firmer pressure as you continue.

* * *

When you're suffering from the sniffles, take a few minutes to do the last shiatzu movement and various others from *60-Second Shiatzu*. You'll want to relax the muscles that ache so much, relieve the blues that so often hit along with the germs, and complete the entire session with a series of shiatzu energizing massages from Chapter 14.

Shiatzu works. Within your fingers you have all the power you need to relieve the symptoms of a cold.

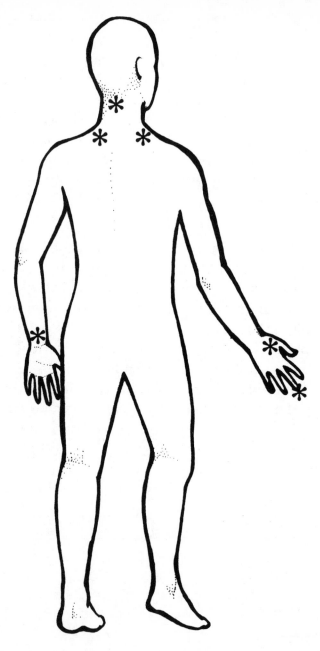

*Location of shiatzu points for Chapter 12 exercises.

CHAPTER

12

Relaxing Moves

Jet lag making you ache? Is it overwork or overplay? Or are you simply feeling like there's just not enough of you to go around? Take a few minutes with shiatzu and relax. Many find they need to be alone for the relaxing moves to do their work. If that's virtually impossible—say you're on a plane to London, or about to speak to the national sales committee,—close your eyes for a moment and regulate your breathing to even increments. When you're ready to begin the shiatzu relaxation moves, rub your hands together briskly until they tingle.

Use your own natural creativity as you work through these moves. Remember, the power is in your own touch. If massage feels okay, but massage combined with a firm amount of pressure works like dynamite, don't be shy, use the pressure massage. The best shiatzu combinations are those moves you feel comfortable doing—so develop a series yourself.

If you're anxious to be on with the business at hand, finish this session with some energizing moves from Chapter 14, and drink a glass of sparkling mineral water or cup of herbal tea to totally re-charge your battery.

• This movement was formulated for *pain* relief. Quite often, your body is experiencing discomfort or a slight ache and that's the reason you can't relax. Without realizing what's happening, you start to feel tense and that tenseness makes relaxation impossible. Don't just pop an aspirin or grin and bear it, instead try this movement. Use other shiatzu moves with it if you need additional relief.

1. Locate the spot on the inside of your forearm about an inch and a half from the wrist fold, closest to the palm.

2. Begin with the fingers of your left hand massaging or bringing gentle pressure to this area on the right arm, and continue for 30 seconds. Repeat the same technique on the left arm. Within 60 seconds you'll notice a difference in your attitude—life's nagging rough spots will seem to smooth, and your sense of humor will return.

* * *

• As explained in the beginning, shiatzu is used on the energy lines of the body called meridians. These massage and pressure points may or may not be right where you'd expect them to be. In the next movement, you'll be massaging the nail area of your middle finger to bring *relief all over*.

1. Take your right hand's middle finger between the index finger and thumb of your left hand.

2. Apply pressure or massage to the lower edge (toward your thumb) of the finger nail. Continue to massage for a count of 15, relax, and repeat on the left middle finger for a count of 15. Repeat the entire sequence for a total of 60 seconds. Make sure your breathing is smooth and measured. Exhale deeply, then inhale from the lower portion of your lungs. Pretend you're at the top of an exquisite mountain and you're drinking in the splendor below.

* * *

• This next movement is worth the "reach across." You'll have to stretch a little, but it's worth the energy expenditure to gain the *relaxation* it will bring. You may want to exhale and inhale as above and close your eyes while you're doing this shiatzu move.

1. With both your right and left elbows pointing to the ceiling, place your fingers on your back and touch your vertebra. Now move your fingers about two inches toward your shoulders. You're not alone if tension seems to accumulate in this area. This spot can be extremely tight or so tender you are unable to use more than your very lightest touch. Go gently at first.

2. Use a circular massage (apply pressure if it's comfortable) for a count of 15, relax, and repeat the techinique for one minute. This movement will feel more natural the more you do it, and it's especially effective when you're suffering from jet lag as it relaxes the back and relieves stiffness in the neck area. It's almost guaranteed to make you feel like you're "in clover" again.

* * *

• Use this movement anytime you **need to relax.** You may want to count backward from ten as you exhale and inhale before doing this move. Deep breathing will help bring the relief you need. There's no definite pattern or iron-clad method for using shiatzu, but the more moves you can memorize, the better your chances will be for improving the quality of your life with shiatzu techniques.

1. Close your eyes, and place the index finger of your left hand on the indentation at the top of your spine, at your hairline on the back of your head. Now allow your chin to rest on your chest.

2. A counter clockwise movement will send relief to your aching, tired body. Massage or apply pressure for a slow count of 15, relax a moment, then repeat this movement for one minute.

* * *

• Anytime you must ''hurry up and wait'' and feel your stress level rising, use this next move. It will *relax* you and relieve the tension that can build up at the back of your neck. It's so easy and inconspicuously done that you can use it in front of your most important client without ever revealing your secret to stress-free success, unless, that is, you want to share.

1. First exhale deeply, wait a moment, then inhale from the lowest portions of your lungs. Place your hands on your lap (under the desk or board table if you prefer) and pinch the fleshy spot on the top of your right hand with your left

thumb and index finger. For extreme tension press hard, for a gentler version apply a counter clockwise massage.

2. Massage or apply pressure for a slow count of 30, relax for a moment, repeat on the left hand. (If you memorize no other moves, engrave this one on your mind—it has hundreds of applications from using it in the dentists' chair to help relieve tension and toothache to helping you cope on a bouncy flight. Since shiatzu only has positive side effects you can continue to treat until you're relaxed.)

Become creative. Mix and match these shiatzu moves with others in the book and develop your own sequence of relaxing movements right now so you can have access to them when you need them.

CHAPTER

13

Shiatzu for Sports

Feeling fit feels great, but along with jogging, aerobic dancing and playing racquet games or the heavy-duty contact variety of sports, can come assorted aches and pains. With shiatzu and the power of your own touch, you can relieve the strain of sports and quickly put your body back in high gear.

Keep in mind that anytime you have prolonged discomfort, excessive swelling or unusual symptoms, you should make a bee line to a sports physician or sports clinic. Exercise should bring benefits to your body—not beat it up.

60-Second Shiatzu will not make you a better athlete. It will help you to help yourself to fitness.

The following moves are dedicated to the competitive as well as to the weekend sports enthusiast. Use them, have fun with them, and incorporate them into your health regimen *today.*

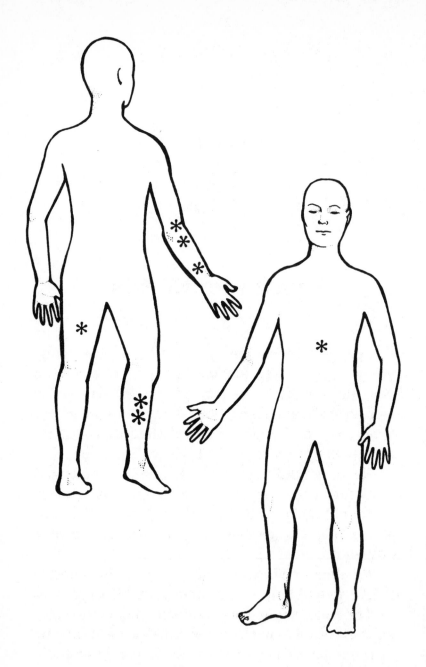

*Location of shiatzu points for Chapter 13 exercises.

• Shiatzu for *tennis elbow:* This tender problem is the result of ligaments being torn or inflamed. For a once-a-month tennis player, it might just be an occasional nuisance—for a super-star of the court, it could be disastrous. Tennis elbow affects golfers, football players, and racquet ball players too, so it makes good sports sense to know the shiatzu point to massage.

1. On the outside of your arm, at the inside fold of the elbow where the arm bends is the spot you'll want to locate. In a sitting position, look down at your elbow crease while your forearm is parallel to the floor. Now place your index finger on the outer end of the crease.

2. Massage or apply pressure to this point on the arm with tennis elbow for a slow count of 30, relax, repeat for another count of 30. This move will also prove to be a plus if you use it morning and night as an addition to your personalized total body shape-up outlined in Chapter 15.

* * *

• For *calf pain:* It's easy to overdo even a good thing like exercise. If you live in a cool climate, the first rush of spring can bring on a bout of sore muscles. Cure your discomfort with shiatzu. The next move is especially designed for tenderness in the lower leg.

1. Locate the shiatzu point about eight inches above the outside ankle bone on the leg with calf tenderness.

2. Massage and apply pressure to this point on the calf for a slow count of 15, relax, exhale and inhale, repeat three more times. You may want to massage for 15 seconds on the right calf then repeat on the left, instead of doing one leg at a time. Try a pulsating massage by simply applying on and off pressure.

* * *

• Weekend athletes suffer with it and so do many in professional competitive sports, especially if they have been out of action for a while due to an injury. For *muscle discomfort* throughout the leg, try this movement.

1. This shiatzu spot is on the back of the thigh halfway between the back of the knee and the fold of your buttocks.

2. Apply counter clockwise massage or pressure to this area on the left leg with the left hand for a slow count of 30, relax, treat the right leg with the right hand for a count of 30. Repeat as necessary. Each leg may need another

treatment, especially if you have over
estimated your flexibility in a vigorous
game.

* * *

• Sometimes feel stiff first thing Monday morning? This movement is a great (and quick) natural aid
that will help you get up and going on those morn-
ings when you would really prefer staying in bed and
letting other people handle the world's business.
Leave the aches and pains to others—you have
shiatzu on your side.

Once you try it, you'll quickly discover this is a
marvelous way to motivate you toward fitness,
especially if you work out after five. For extra energy,
rub your hands together briskly, then proceed with
the massage.

Try the next movement for the *overall stiffness*
that sometimes hits "the day after." This two-part
shiatzu massage will be an excellent addition to your
regular fitness regimen or to enhance your stretching
program for any sport.

1. Locate the point on the outside of the
   calf about four inches below the knee
   bend. Apply pressure or massage to this
   point for a count of 30. Relax, repeat on
   the other calf, then begin step 2.

2. Apply counter clockwise pressure or pulsating massage at the web of the thumb and index finger, first on the right hand using your left thumb and index finger for a count of 30, then on the left hand for another count of 30. Make sure your breathing is deep and relaxed as you use shiatzu to revitalize those over-played muscles.

* * *

• Are you an aerobic dancer? A twenty-mile a week walker or runner? Do you push those free weights around the gym? Regardless of your fitness routine, there are times when you want to almost instantly prepare your body to move. This shiatzu treatment will help you do just that because it *energizes your whole body.* Each of the steps takes about 60 seconds and it's truly a dynamite trio if you're serious about feeling and looking great.

You can use these movements in the locker room at the fitness center or standing at the track. With shiatzu as part of your fitness plan, you never have to feel out-of-step, and you can do all the moves in your sweats, leotard or running shorts—why, you can even do them in your business suit in the privacy of your office just before you head out the door for the track or gym.

These movements will definitely enhance any workout, but "trying is believing," so give it a tumble.

This is a three-part plan and seems to be more beneficial for athletes when played by the numbers.

1. Locate the shiatzu point at the "pit" of the stomach, between the breast bone and the navel. Slowly count to 15 while applying clockwise massage or pressure, relax for a moment, repeat three more times before you proceed to step 2.

2. About 2 1/2 inches from the wrist fold, on the top of the arm, is the shiatzu point you'll want to locate for this move. Touch your arm and find the spot between the two tendons in your forearm. Apply pressure or clockwise massage on the right arm for a slow count of 15. Relax, repeat the treatment on the left arm. Now repeat the entire procedure for step 2 before you go on to step 3.

3. You'll find this spot about 1 1/2 inches below the elbow crease on the top of the forearm toward the wrist. Gently separate the muscles and feel for a tightness. If you're stressed there may be a "knot" in this area. Massage or apply pressure with the left hand to the spot for a slow count of 15, relax, repeat on the left arm. Relax for a moment and do both arms again.

It's as easy as that. Use shiatzu to tune you up and energize every part of you. It's a drug-free stimulant and great for any body.

CHAPTER

14

Super Energizers

Don't pour another cup of coffee or grab a chocolate bar to increase your energy. Instead, use the next series of shiatzu moves to boost your stamina, maintain your strength, and push your creativity sky high.

Revitalize your body any minute of the day and just watch the competition stand back and shake their heads in dismay while you charge toward the top.

While energizing with shiatzu, use the techniques you already know, such as exhaling deeply and inhaling through your nose for a moment or two before performing the moves, rubbing your hands together as if warming them on a cold morning, and straightening your posture. To get lasting energy you don't need to rely on recreational drugs; that energy is always within you, waiting for you to unleash it. With the shiatzu *super energizers*, that lasting energy is as close as the power of your own touch.

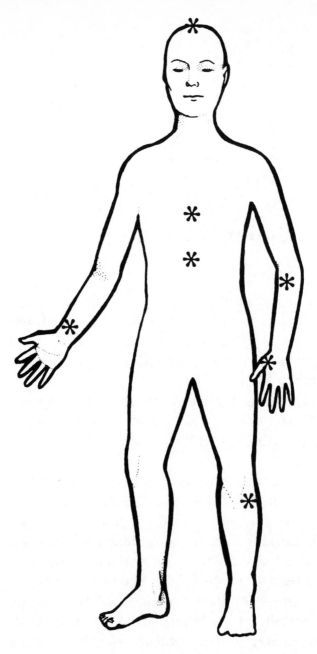

*Location of shiatzu points for Chapter 14 exercises.

Do the following ***super energizers*** in a series, or select the ones that feel most natural to you. You're an individual in everything you do and you'll probably react uniquely to the energizers. Try them all and incorporate any you like from other chapters into the exercises in this section. Your health is your personal responsibility, and it's up to you to make shiatzu work.

• You'll probably want to add this shiatzu move to your growing list of "favorites," especially if you travel and have to cope with jet lag, "red eye specials," or routinely burn the midnight oil. Take a moment to listen to your body. Begin by exhaling deeply, closing your eyes, then slowly inhaling. If you're unable to ***relax***, imagine yourself totally serene yet excited, standing atop a spectacular mountain crest. Pretend it's the season you like best and the air is crisp. As you inhale, drink in that freshness and feel it generate abundant energy for every cell in your body.

Both of these moves are done in a sitting position—at your desk, in a traffic jam, anywhere and anytime you need to boost your energy level. They are excellent as part of your bedtime routine—make them a habit just like brushing your teeth and you'll wake refreshed.

1. Bring the thumb and fingers of your right hand close together. In the very fleshy

spot on top of your hand, where the crease stops between the thumb and index finger, is the shiatzu point you'll massage. With the thumb or index finger of your left hand apply clockwise massage or a pulsating pressure at this point for a slow count of 15. Relax, repeat the same move on your left hand. Now continue with the second part of this energizer.

2. Sitting with feet flat on the floor, slip your left hand into the 90 degree angle of your right leg, with thumb under the bend. Place your fingers around the front of your knee, and make an imaginary line from the middle finger to a spot on the outside of your calf, about four or five inches from the top of your knee. Massage or apply pressure to this point for 15 seconds before repeating the move on the right leg.

Finish the movements with a moment or two of deep breathing as you did before starting the exercise, and "go get 'em, Tiger!"

* * *

• Want to feel really sensational and"fine-tuned?" Combine all the *super energizers* with aerobic exercise and keep your diet low in fat, salt, and refined sugar. Allow shiatzu to enhance your healthstyle (all the things you do to keep yourself healthy) and use the following moves when you feel your mind's hazy, you can't concentrate, or you simply want to **recharge** your creativity.

These take a total of three minutes and are to be done in a sitting position. Read through the simple directions, close your eyes, and begin by gently massaging your shoulders, neck, and upper arms. Proceed to step 1.

1. Place the fingers of your left hand at the "pit" of the stomach—between the breast bone and navel. Apply a clockwise pressure for 30 seconds. Exhale deeply, and inhale as you go on to the second part.

2. Place the fingers of your left hand at the center of your chest, between your nipples. Apply a clockwise massage or pulsating pressure for a slow count of 30.

3. To complete this energizer, measure about the width of eight fingers above your eyebrows by placing the little finger of your right hand on your eyebrows and laying your hand flat on your forehead with fingers together. Now put your left hand, also with fingers together and flat, right above it. Where your index finger

is placed, at the top center of your head, is the spot you'll want to massage with a clockwise pressure or pulsating touch. Continue for a slow count of 30. Exhale, and inhale deeply.

Repeat all three steps three times. Feel the difference? You bet!

* * *

• Let shiatzu come to your aid when you need to energize but can't get out to sweat. The following moves are sensational for revitalizing your memory. When your thinking is clear and concise, you naturally feel at your best. Perform the following series in a comfortable sitting position if possible, but they work well done in any position.

1. Place the fingers of your left hand on the top of your head. Apply a pulsating or clockwise massage for a slow count of 15, relax, repeat.

2. Put the index and middle fingers of your left hand at the "pit" of your stomach, right between the breast bone and the navel. Apply a clockwise massage for a slow count of 30, then proceed with the last part of this exercise.

3. Locate this point on the inside of the forearm about 1 1/2 inches from the wrist fold on the palm side. As you touch your arm, you'll feel the two tendons. Apply pressure or clockwise massage to this spot for a slow count of 15, relax, and repeat on the other arm. Do the entire series of moves two more times.

* * *

• Need a quick pick-me-up? Try this routine.

1. Touch your forearm muscles about 1 1/2 inches below the elbow crease, toward the wrist on the outside of the arm. Apply a clockwise or a pulsating massage for a slow count of 15 to the right arm, then switch to the left arm.

2. Apply pressure on the forearm about 1 1/2 inches above the wrist fold on the palm side. Apply a gentle massage between the two tendons on your right arm, then switch to the left arm. Massage each arm for a slow count of 15.

3. Place the fingers of your left hand on the "pit" of your stomach, between the navel and the breast bone. Massage in a clockwise direction for a slow count of 30.

Repeat all three moves two more times. Exhale slowly and completely, then inhale deeply, first filling the lower portion of your lungs.

The *super energizers* are the perfect solution when you want to completely recharge all of you— body, mind, and determination. Familiarize yourself with the moves right now so that when you need that extra energy boost, it'll be as close as your fingertips.

CHAPTER

15

Total Body Shape Up

Within one minute shiatzu can send energy pulsating throughout your body. Here's your chance to do more with the power of your touch than merely use these great moves when you're tense, tired, or tuned out. Utilize the techniques every morning before your feet hit the floor, then go through another routine in the evening when you're ready to rest. Make shiatzu a regular addition to your life.

• The first exercise should be done in bed and is a combination of movements that will take 60 seconds for each part. Don't hesitate to repeat the whole exercise. You can't overdose on shiatzu, so if it feels good it is good for you.

1. With the thumbs of both hands locate the indentations at the back of your head to the sides of your spinal column. Fan your

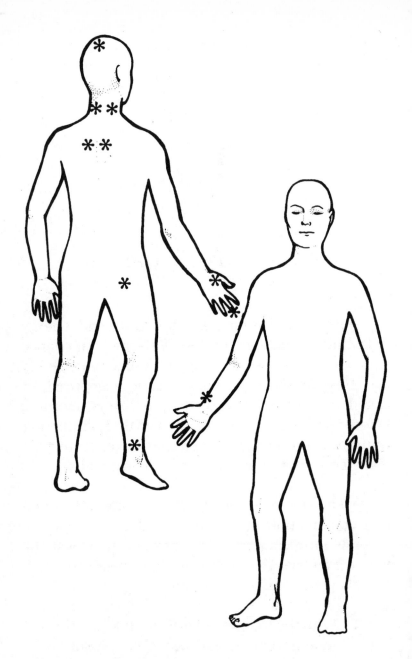

*Location of shiatzu points for Chapter 15 exercises.

fingers out at the sides of your head as you massage with your thumbs for a slow count of 30, relax, and repeat.

2. Locate the mid-point between the eyebrows and the base of your skull at the very top of your head. Apply clockwise or pulsating pressure to this point for a slow count of 30, relax, exhale, inhale deeply, and repeat.

3. Lying on your right hip and using your left hand, massage at a point about four inches below the top of your hip bone in the fleshy part of the left buttock. Use clockwise or pulsating massage for a slow count of 30, relax, roll on your left hip, repeat the move on the right side.

* * *

• This two-part shiatzu movement will help restore your confidence as it erases any *sluggishness* in your mind. It's an excellent move when done before you climb out of bed.

1. Lying on your back, bring your feet close to the buttocks and place your fingers on each ankle bone. Now measure about four inches up from the ankle bones on the outsides of the legs. At these points, apply clockwise massage or pressure for a slow count of 30, relax, and repeat.

2. Still lying on your back, use your left hand to massage the web between the thumb and index finger on your right hand. A pulsating or circular massage technique with this move works well. Do it for a slow count of 30 before proceeding to the left hand.

* * *

• Relaxing at the end of a busy day isn't always easy, yet when you're familiar with the comforting moves of shiatzu, there's no need to resort to artificial relaxants or alcohol. *Relax* naturally with the next two moves. Make them a regular part of your health-oriented lifestyle. Both moves are done in a relaxed position with eyes closed.

1. Using your left hand, place your fingers on the outside wrist fold of the palm side of your right hand. Massage in a counter clockwise direction for a count of 15, relax, repeat on the left wrist for another slow count of 15.

2. Place the fingers of both hands on the crown of your head. Fan the fingers slightly. Now using all your fingers, apply pressure or massage to the head for a count of 15, release, allow head to come forward and rest lightly on your chest.

Take a deep breath and repeat for another count of 15.

Use these moves in the evening, but also give them a try before you leave work so you can keep your mind on the traffic, yet feel fine when you walk through the front door.

If you have decided you really want to lose those extra pounds and think nervous snacking accounts for your present weight, try the previous exercise. It will help you to approach your weight-loss plan relaxed and feeling positive about yourself.

* * *

• It's not unusual to feel *"used up"* at the end of a hectic day. "You're not alone" really doesn't help, either. What will help is this next two-part move which takes about four minutes. Memorize it. You'll want to use it often.

1. Take your right hand's middle finger between the index finger and thumb of your left hand. Apply pulsating pressure to the lower edge of the finger nail, toward the thumb. Continue to massage for a count of 30, relax, and repeat on the other hand. Exhale deeply, and slowly replace the air in your lungs, starting with the lowest portion. Repeat the first part of this movement.

2. With both your right and left elbows pointed toward the ceiling, place your fingers on your back and touch your vertebra. Move your hands about two inches toward the sides and apply a counter clockwise massage for a count of 30, relax, breathe deeply, and repeat three more times.

* * *

Read through the shiatzu moves listed in previous chapters. If you need to energize, do one move from Chapter 14, plus the first two in this chapter. Feel a deep ache in the shoulder and neck? Try a move from Chapter 4, and one of the relaxing moves above. Headache? Flip to Chapter 2 and select a move that's natural to you, then add a revitalizing or relaxing move. The choices are only limited by your time and creativity. The price is definitely right, and you're in charge of your body all the time.

Make shiatzu work with the power of your own touch. Do it every day, morning and night—you'll feel better for it.

16

Yesterday, Today, and Tomorrow

Shiatzu's goal is to promote health—physical and mental.

The Japanese were first to introduce acupuncture, the insertion of needles into the meridians which control the flow of energy, to treat illness in the body, about thirteen hundred years ago. Taking it a step further, they blended the use of touch, instead of needles, and the traditional amma form of Oriental massage to formulate the healing art of shiatzu. Those ancient teachers rightly believed that pressure on the acupuncture meridians or pressure points would bring about the same positive results without puncturing the body.

That's the first recorded history of shiatzu, but applying pressure to a tender spot or a wound goes back to the beginning of mankind. Consider for a moment the natural response when you hurt yourself. Don't you instinctively rub the area—applying pressure? Without thinking about what you are doing, you use a method of shiatzu or acupressure to help restore health.

People have done exactly that for thousands of years, by applying pressure to stop bleeding, rubbing an irritated area, and massaging sore muscles, they discovered relief. Shiatzu is an offshoot of this prehistoric technique.

Tales about the wonders of shiatzu circulated throughout ancient Japan. Early practitioners learned and shared the health-saving methods of simply pressing and rubbing painful spots on the bodies of their patients with the palms and fingers. But according to this ancient story, the power of touch can do more than restore energy.

* * *

Once upon a time in old Japan a young woman who was very upset and disgusted with her elderly mother-in-law decided to do away with the old lady. She traveled out into the countryside to visit the local medical practitioner. He gave the woman a poison and explained a method of touching the old shrew which would bring the relief she wanted—eliminating the mother-in-law permanently from her life.

The sage, who had given the treatment, was a wise and worldly man. After weeks of giving the treatment and the liquid to her mother-in-law, the woman abruptly changed her mind. How could she do away with the old lady? She rushed to the practitioner for an antidote with which to undo the damage.

The story goes that the liquid was merely rosewater. And the curse? Shiatzu movements. By bringing their lives together through shiatzu, both found the balance they needed.

* * *

There are more than sixteen theories as to exactly why shiatzu, acupressure, and acupuncture work. Eastern and Western medical practitioners are still in conflict—yet it does work, and when you want to energize and promote your own health, that's the bottom line.

Following Oriental philosophy, one theory is that throughout the universe and flowing within each of us is a force which is called ''chi'' or ''ki.'' This force may become unbalanced or stopped when a person is not attuned to life. Shiatzu can unblock and restore health as the chi or ki is again able to move freely within the body.

Discuss this with a Western medical specialist and you'll probably get a raised eyebrow or two. Western medical practitioners believe that shiatzu, acupressure, and acupuncture work because the needles or pressure stimulate the autonomic nervous system and promote health in this way.

Basically, the energy in the body flows through fourteen pathways called ''meridians.'' Twelve meridians are paired in the body as a mirror image. The remaining two are the conception vessel which runs centrally on the front of the body, and the governing vessel which parallels the conception vessel on the back. The meridians for these vessels are connected at the pelvis and above the upper lip. Each meridian has a name or reference to a bodily organ such as bladder, kidney, and colon, however, there is no physical relationship between the meridian and the organs or functions after which they're named.

Reviewing a book on shiatzu, or acupressure, you'll see the pressure points abbreviated, such as Gb20—which is the 20th point on the Gall Bladder meridian, although it's not directly related to the gall bladder in any way. Shiatzu therapists and acupuncturists use this system today. The French were the first to bring shiatzu into respectable European thinking and developed this "shorthand" method for identifying the pressure points. Originally this method used two Chinese characters, which sometimes located a point—sometimes a traditional function. After the translation and streamlining of the system, some of the ancient meanings of the characters were lost.

When discussing a shiatzu treatment, the practitioner may explain the imbalances in the body and massage according to the meridians and the abbreviated point identification system used worldwide today.

The future? It's wide open for shiatzu and a full range of traditional healing methods. Holistic practitioners, nurse practitioners, RN's, midwives, and physicians are now keenly interested and beginning to use the ancient methods, and combining them with high-tech health and science procedures. (See Chapter 17 for more insight on the role of shiatzu in Western medicine.) The possibility of shiatzu's changing the way people treat themselves is significant. Many shiatzu therapists feel that within the next ten years, this ancient non-drug method will be a well-established part of health care with your health insurance covering the cost of treatment.

Medical discoveries surface everyday, and theories abound, not only in the USA and the Orient, on how shiatzu really works. Pressure massage has become an established alternative healing method in the Soviet Union, Canada, England, France, Italy, and a score of other countries. There are over a thousand points known and charted which when pressed or massaged can bring relief from pain and increase the body's ability to heal itself. The ones offered in **60-Second Shiatzu** are the basics of this revitalizing system.

As you can imagine, shiatzu therapists devote years to studying the pressure points, spending extended periods of their lives in apprenticeships. The method discussed here is for instant self-help, relaxation, and revitalization. With these exercises you'll be able to free your body from tension, energize, and assume responsibility for your future healthstyle.

✳ ✳ ✳

CHAPTER

17

Shiatzu—A Safe and Sane Alternative

Shiatzu isn't intended to be a cure for every ailment, but is a drug-free, positive, habit-forming energizer, relaxer, pain eraser, and revitalizer for the whole body, right now, today, without a prescription or lengthy set of instructions.

Since there is no risk of infection or rupture, as with acupuncture, shiatzu is the perfect choice, especially if you consider your health to be your personal responsibility. You can do for yourself on yourself.

In recent years, acupressure and other forms of shiatzu have been used increasingly, and with outstanding success, as a method to control pain during minor operations in the oro-maxillofacial area, as documented by the Department of Oral and Maxillofacial Surgery, Sichuan Medical College, Chengdu, People's Republic of China.

The *American Journal of Acupuncture,* August 1980, reported that acupressure and shiatzu massage had been used effectively in a community health education center over a period of six years with amazing results. According to the journal, the center provided an eight-session instruction course which included neuroanatomical and physiological theory of the body's functions and practical exercises taught in a group format. The goal was safe self-management of pain and stiffness due to physical and/or physiological, and stress-related conditions.

A 24-month study in *Current Psychiatric Therapy,* (1977), documented the successful treatment of headache pain with "auto-acupressure." The acupressure or shiatzu techniques were evaluated as symptomatic treatment for the pain of migraine, allergy, and tension headaches. The study was conducted with more than 500 neuropsychiatric outpatients, seen for more than 5000 visits. More than 200, according to the article, had significant headaches—occurring more than once a week. The results? "Auto-acupressure" replaced outpatient prescriptions for analgesics and stronger medications, and the physicians involved felt that the value of this alternative health method was greatly enhanced by its easy availability and lack of toxic effects.

The *American Journal of Chinese Medicine,* (1982), in an article titled "Preventive Geriatrics an Overview From Traditional Chinese Medicine," stated that various methods, including acupressure were helpful in improving the general health of the elderly *and* in promoting longevity.

The California Nurses Association's official bulletin, *California Nurse,* (January 1985), discussed the "growing number of proponents" who are taking a closer look at holistic health care, including shiatzu, and it's already an established part of treatment for many patients seen by holistic physicians and hospital nursing staff members.

Ethical, licensed medical practitioners (M.D.'s), home nursing staff members, and hospital nurses are using shiatzu and other forms of acupressure on their patients on a daily basis with excellent results. Documentation is becoming available that supports shiatzu and acupressure as a viable alternative, and credit is being given as part of continuing education courses for RN's. Shiatzu is even being used in schools to promote well-being, especially with children who have learning disabilities. It's supplementing existing medical practices on a growing variety of levels.

For additional background material, refer to the bibliography. For additional practice in revitalizing your entire body, start now with *60-Second Shiatzu*.

CHAPTER

18

Locating a Shiatzu Therapist

Once you become comfortable with self-administered shiatzu, the natural next step may be to seek out a shiatzu therapist for a professional treatment.

A complete shiatzu massage done by an experienced therapist is like comparing home cooking with gourmet cuisine. Yes, homemade is wholesome and it's good for you, but when food is prepared by a creative culinary genius, it's a gastronomical delight. Consider a total body shiatzu treatment in the same way—something you can relish and enjoy. But be warned, you might become addicted.

If you go to a therapist expecting to meet an ancient Oriental in a violet kimono, you'll be greatly disappointed. Most are career people just like you, although theirs is a service field. Many are trained as physicians, osteopaths, chiropractors, and nurses; however, there are students on the beginning level who do shiatzu massage, too. In some cities, massage therapists must have a license. In others they can just "hang out a shingle."

Actually it's a lot like selecting a doctor or a hairdresser when you've moved to another city. You start by making initial inquiries among friends, asking around the office, checking the phone book, and skimming through those "alternative" newspapers which always seem to be underfoot at the record store. If there's a holistic (sometimes spelled "wholistic") health center in your community, that's probably the easiest place to start.

Before you make an appointment, if possible, talk with the therapist on the phone. At the very least talk to someone in the office to find out what you'll get for your money. Here are some questions to ask and reasons why the answers are important to you:

1. What is the therapist's background? The therapist may have been trained in Japan by a master or at the local shiatzu therapy school. If a therapist has a medical background that's great, but don't discount one who has been practicing for years and has a fine reputation.

You can expect answers something like, "I'm a registered nurse with extensive education in all forms of massage therapy, but I feel shiatzu brings about the most positive benefits in life." If the response is vague, "I've been doing this for a while," it'll be up to you as the consumer to decide if you want to accept an appointment with no more information about background than that.

Feel free to ask more specific questions such as: Where were you trained? How long have you been practicing? Can I have the names and phone numbers of a few references?

2. What is your fee for a shiatzu massage? The price of a total shiatzu massage done by a therapist with extensive experience and/or a medical degree can range from £15 per session up. The cost of a session will depend on your city and the expertise of the therapist. For someone fresh out of therapist training, you may be able to have a massage for as little as £10.

Just because the price is high, doesn't necessarily mean you'll get a better massage, so continue your questions with...

3. What will the treatment entail? There are no "typical" standards, but probably the shiatzu massage will take about one hour, maybe more for the first session. You'll probably want to take three sessions over a three to six-week period. Ask the therapist for moves you can do at home to enhance the ones in *60-Second Shiatzu.*

Don't be surprised if you and the therapist simply sit quietly for a few minutes discussing your life, how you feel about yourself, and exactly what you hope to gain from a shiatzu massage. He or she will want to know you as a whole person.

A shiatzu therapist will want to become familiar with your health-style, whether you're in a high-stress career, how you cope with tension, your nutritional philosophy, and generally gather as much

121

insight as possible into what makes you tick. He's not just nosey, although it may seem that way if you're a reserved individual. It's through this information that the therapist can "prescribe" changes in your total fitness plan that will bring you greater rewards than merely having him/her massage and work the pressure points in your body.

If you feel awkward about having the massage only covered by a sheet, speak up, and ask that the massage be done with you fully clothed. Most therapists ask you to disrobe while they're out of the room (leaving on your underwear), then during the massage they only expose the part of your body on which they're working, while keeping the rest of you covered with a sheet. If this concerns you, find out about it while you're making your appointment so you'll have no surprises when you get to the office.

4. What techniques will be used? For the definition of some shiatzu terms, refer to the glossary at the end of this chapter since the therapist will probably use the words to describe the treatment. If this is your first massage, tell the therapist and remember that you'll profit more from the experience if you ask questions and understand the answers.

As you'll quickly learn, each shiatzu therapist is unique in his or her approach to massage, so the following is only meant as an overview, an approximation of what you'll experience. For "first timers" it will help you to understand the procedure so you can relax and enjoy it.

The therapist will probably begin by having you lie on your back and will give you a light, all-over shiatzu massage to discover any sensitive points on your body. Then the therapist may massage the abdomen and chest, go on to the neck and head, followed by the shoulder area, before you roll over. Lying on your stomach, the shoulders, neck, arms, and back will be massaged, before moving down to the hips, backs of legs, and feet. Finally, the therapist may have you turn on your back, to work the front of your legs, and end with the neck area.

The therapist may "warm up" the area to be massaged by using a light rubbing technique, then do a heavier pressure massage before completing the area treatment with a soothing, gentle rubbing or stroking. The entire session is as relaxing as a sigh and should never cause you pain or discomfort. If it does, tell the therapist.

Relax, most shiatzu therapists are concerned only with your well-being and if at any time you feel inhibited or embarrassed, speak up. He or she will not work any part of your body not directly concerned with the treatment.

Massage and pressure of the shiatzu points are normally centered in the areas of:

The head.

The neck.

The shoulders and arms, including the hands.

The back.

The front and rear of the calf and thigh.

The feet.

✳ ✳ ✳

Glossary of Shiatzu Terms

To keep communication clear between you and the therapist, here's a brief listing of terms he or she may use.

Acupressure: The use of pressure on meridians, or energy channels in the body, to enhance health. Shiatzu is a form of acupressure.

Acupuncture: The use of needles at meridian points, inserted into the body, to bring about health in the patient.

Body Work: Any form of massage, including shiatzu, rolfing, and acupressure.

Chi or Ki: The energy force balancing the body and the universe.

Japanese Shiatzu: A form of shiatzu which may include deep, sometimes painful, body work as the therapist uses pressure to manipulate the patient.

Massage: Working or kneading the flesh of a person either by a second person or through self-manipulation.

Meridian: An energy channel, one of many, which shiatzu advocates believe govern the health of an individual. By applying pressure on these meridians at certain points, the body is able to release blockages and re-establish a healthy balance.

Meridian Symbols: The following are the symbols used to identify various pressure points in the body and the flow of the universal energy source, called 'Chi'' or''Ki''. Consider the meridians as a road map and not associated with the organ or function after which they're named.

Lg: Lung meridian flowing from the chest to the hand.

Co: Colon meridian flowing from the hand to the face.

St: Stomach meridian flowing from the face to the foot and down the foot.

Sp: Spleen-pancreas meridian flowing from the foot to the chest.

Ht: Heart meridian flowing from the chest to the hand.

Si: Small intestine meridian flowing from the head to the hand.

Bl: Bladder meridian flowing from the face, down the body to the feet.

Ki: Kidney meridian flowing from the foot to the chest.

Cs: Circulation-sex meridian flowing from the chest to the hand.

Th: Triple heater meridian flowing from the hand to the face.

Gb: Gall bladder meridian flowing from the face to the foot.

Lv: Liver meridian flowing from the foot to the chest.

Vc: Vessel of conception, front midline of the body.

Gv: Governing vessel, back midline of the body.

Polarity Therapy: A combination of rolfing and acupressure where there is concentrated pressure applied with a knuckle, thumb, or elbow to bring alignment of posture.

Proskauer Massage: Developed by Magda Proskauer, is a subtle form of massage currently known as breath therapy. The feather-light massage is timed with the breathing cycle. It was designed to increase awareness and promote health.

Rolfing: A deep form of body massage, ordinarily taking ten sessions, which many find extremely painful, yet exhilarating. Many say they have more energy, a greater sense of well-being, and a more positive outlook on life after being "rolfed."

Shiatzu: Massage of acupuncture points combined with the traditional amma form of Oriental massage ("am" meaning press and "ma" meaning stroke).

60-Second Shiatzu: An innovative self-help program used as "first aid" to health, as a method to revitalize almost instantly and to increase the powerful, positive energy flowing within the body while promoting awareness and balance in contemporary life.

Yin and Yang: The opposing but complementary forces which Chinese philosophers believe balance everything in the universe.

Zone Therapy or Reflexology: The theory that every organ and muscle has a corresponding point on the feet. To locate and treat problems affecting the body, you locate the points on the feet and massage.

Australian Shiatsu Organisations and Courses

New South Wales: **Sydney Shiatsu Centre**, 2nd Floor, 215a Thomas Street, Sydney 2000. Tel: (02) 212 3515

Offers shiatsu massage and courses.

Victoria: **Australian Shiatsu College**, P.O. Box 1188, Collingwood 3065. Tel: (03) 419 5520.

Offers shiatsu therapy and education.